human rights *first*

Living in Limbo

Iraqi Refugees and U.S. Resettlement

December 2010

About Human Rights First

Human Rights First believes that building respect for human rights and the rule of law will help ensure the dignity to which every individual is entitled and will stem tyranny, extremism, intolerance, and violence.

Human Rights First protects people at risk: refugees who flee persecution, victims of crimes against humanity or other mass human rights violations, victims of discrimination, those whose rights are eroded in the name of national security, and human rights advocates who are targeted for defending the rights of others. These groups are often the first victims of societal instability and breakdown; their treatment is a harbinger of wider-scale repression. Human Rights First works to prevent violations against these groups and to seek justice and accountability for violations against them.

Human Rights First is practical and effective. We advocate for change at the highest levels of national and international policymaking. We seek justice through the courts. We raise awareness and understanding through the media. We build coalitions among those with divergent views. And we mobilize people to act.

Human Rights First is a non-profit, non-partisan international human rights organization based in New York and Washington D.C. To maintain our independence, we accept no government funding.

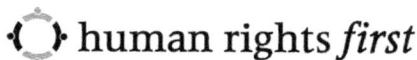

human rights *first*

Headquarters

333 Seventh Avenue
13th Floor
New York, NY 10001-5108

Tel.: 212.845.5200
Fax: 212.845.5299

Washington D.C. Office

100 Maryland Avenue, NE
Suite 500
Washington, DC 20002-5625

Tel: 202.547.5692
Fax: 202.543.5999

www.humanrightsfirst.org

This report is available for free online at www.humanrightsfirst.org

Acknowledgements

This report is primarily based on research in Egypt, Jordan, Lebanon, Geneva, New York and Washington, D.C. conducted between April and November 2010, including approximately fifty interviews with Iraqi refugees in Lebanon, Jordan, Egypt and New York. This report was researched and written by Jesse Bernstein, Ruthie Epstein, Sara Faust and Parastou Hassouri, a consultant to Human Rights First. Additional research, writing, editing and/or comments were provided by Eleanor Acer, Reena Arya, Anwen Hughes, Robyn Lieberman, Annie Sovcik and Tad Stahnke.

The authors are grateful to the many individuals, organizations and agencies who provided time, information and insights during the course of our research. In particular, the authors wish to thank the many refugees and pro bono attorneys interviewed, as well as the various U.S. and other government officials and UNHCR staff who met with us during our research and/or provided comments on this report. We also wish to thank CARE Jordan, the International Catholic Migration Commission (ICMC) in Jordan, the Danish Refugee Council in Lebanon, International Relief and Development in Jordan and Africa and Middle East Assistance (AMERA) Egypt for their hospitality and facilitating of visits.

Human Rights First wishes to express its appreciation to Robert Pennoyer and the donors to the Pennoyer Fellowship for creating the program that supports Mr. Bernstein's position at Human Rights First. We also wish to thank Human Rights First's general support donors—both foundations and individuals—who make our research and advocacy possible.

Contents

Summary and Key Findings

Just a few months after President Obama declared the end to the United States combat mission in Iraq, security remains erratic in many parts of the country. In October of this year, approximately 50 individuals were killed after armed militants stormed Our Lady of Salvation Church in central Baghdad during Sunday mass.[1] Following this attack, in early November, 63 civilians were killed in a series of explosions throughout Baghdad.[2] These and other brutal attacks, along with the prolonged difficulties in forming a government, are recent reminders that, despite improvements in security in Iraq, long-term stability in the country remains elusive and many Iraqis remain at risk.

Iraqis who flee today join other Iraqi refugees in neighboring countries who are struggling to survive with limited ability to exercise their basic rights. Since the beginning of the war, the majority of Iraqis have fled to Syria and Jordan. Thousands of others now live in Turkey, Lebanon, Egypt and other countries in the region. Over 30,000 Iraqi refugees registered with the U.N. refugee agency (UNHCR) in these countries during 2010 alone, including some 3,000 new registrations in Syria and Jordan in the month of October.[3] A total of 195,428 Iraqi refugees are currently registered with UNHCR in the region.[4] while an unknown number of additional refugees have not registered or let their registrations lapse. Though Iraq's neighbors have generously hosted hundreds of thousands of Iraqi refugees, the majority of Iraqi refugees have no access to formal legal status or employment authorization. Without these basic forms of protection, many of these refugees are unable to support their families and live at constant risk of arrest, detention and possible deportation. For these and other reasons, most Iraqi refugees have no hope of integrating in these countries.

While a small portion of Iraqis have returned—or attempted to return—to Iraq, Iraqis are still fleeing their country due to the continuing violence, persecution, insecurity and lack of access to basic services. A recent UNHCR survey found that Iraqis who had returned to Baghdad from neighboring countries experienced high levels of violence after their return—including explosions, kidnappings and other violent incidents.[5] Most of these Iraqis regretted their decisions to return, and some were considering whether to flee the country yet again. With neither return to Iraq, nor local integration, as realistic possibilities, resettlement to third countries is essential in providing many Iraqi refugees with sustainable and long-term solutions to their displacement.

In this report, Human Rights First documents a number of persistent problems that are undermining the effectiveness of the resettlement and special immigrant visa (SIV) programs through which some Iraqis are able to legally come to and permanently stay in the United States. While there have been some real improvements in the processing of Iraqi resettlement applications to the United States over the last three years, significant delays and inefficiencies remain. Many of these processing delays—including those caused by inadequate staffing to process security checks—are not new. In fact, over three years ago, former U.S. Ambassador to Iraq Ryan Crocker complained about the "bottlenecks" in Iraqi refugee processing and asked that the lengthy waiting times for security checks be reduced substantially.[6] Human Rights First's interviews and research demonstrate that while some Iraqi refugees wait for extended periods—sometimes as long as two years—they are left stranded in difficult or dangerous circumstances. These delays and inefficiencies also undermine the effectiveness of the U.S. refugee resettlement program, as well as two programs that Congress—in bi-partisan legislation—created to ensure that U.S.-affiliated Iraqis are brought to safety quickly. As detailed below, fixing these problems is both a moral obligation and a strategic imperative for the United States.

The Threat of Persecution in Iraq

While many Iraqis remain at risk of violence within Iraqi, different groups of Iraqis continue to face targeted persecution. The persecution of religious minorities has been extensively documented, including by the bi-partisan United States Commission on International Religious Freedom.[7] The horrific attacks on the Christian communities in October and November confirm that religious minorities continue to face grave risks in Iraq.[8] Other minorities, including sexual minorities, also face targeted violence in Iraq.

Iraqis employed by U.S. entities also continue to face threats and violence due to their affiliation with the United States. Those Iraqis who chose to work for the U.S. government, military or contractors, or for U.S.-based media groups or non-governmental organizations—who were crucially important to provide local expertise and language skills to the Americans—were quickly labeled as traitors by different militia groups inside Iraq.

The threats these Iraqis have faced—from insurgent groups, militias and terrorist organizations—have been well documented in the media. While the levels of violence are not as high as they were during the peak of the sectarian violence, as detailed in Section III of this report, these individuals remain at risk.

The Bi-partisan Effort to Assist Iraqi Refugees and U.S.-Affiliated Iraqis

The initial U.S. response to the plight of Iraqi refugees fell far short of the kind of leadership role the United States is capable of playing to address refugee crises—and distressingly short given the United States' central role in the Iraq war itself and its deep debt to the Iraqis who had placed their lives at risk by working with Americans. Many observers argued that addressing the plight of Iraq's refugees was not only a moral obligation of the United

States, but also a strategic imperative. For example, the bi-partisan Iraq Study Group, co-chaired by James Baker (former Secretary of State under President George H.W. Bush) and Lee Hamilton (former Democratic congressman from Indiana), pointed out in its December 2006 report that "[if the Iraqi refugee crisis] is not addressed, Iraq and the region could be further destabilized, and the humanitarian suffering could be severe."[9]

In June 2007, Senator Edward Kennedy (D-MA) and Senator Gordon Smith (R-OR) introduced the bi-partisan Refugee Crisis in Iraq Act. The bill was aimed at improving the response of the United States to the plight of Iraq's refugees and ensuring that Iraqis who had worked with the U.S. government, military and contractors, as well as with the U.S. media or other groups, were provided with effective routes of escape to ensure their protection. The legislation proposed by Senators Kennedy and Smith received broad bi-partisan support, passed the Senate unanimously that fall, and was signed into law on January 28, 2008, as part of the Department of Defense Authorization Act for Fiscal Year 2008. Senator Smith spoke of "a national moral commitment" to resolving the Iraqi refugee issue.[10] Senator Carl Levin (D-MI), Chairman of the Senate Armed Services Committee, similarly stressed that "the United States has a moral obligation to help those Iraqis who have assisted or are assisting our military and civilian forces."[11] President Bush affirmed this commitment when he signed the Refugee Crisis in Iraq Act into law in February 2008.

The Refugee Crisis in Iraq Act—which is described in detail in Section III of this report—committed the United States to take more decisive action to address the needs of Iraq's refugees and to create a set of programs to provide routes of escape to the United States for U.S.-affiliated Iraqis facing danger inside Iraq.

One year later, the newly elected President Obama recognized all Iraqi refugee and internally displaced families as "living consequence[s] of this war" and affirmed that "America has a strategic interest—and a moral responsibility—to act."[12]

U.S. Leadership and Progress

Over the last three years, the U.S. government has significantly improved its efforts to address the needs of Iraq's refugees and displaced persons. The United States has played a leadership role in providing humanitarian assistance for Iraq's refugees and displaced persons, as well as contributed significantly to UNHCR's Iraqi refugee operations. The United States has also encouraged other countries to increase their support for Iraqi refugees and displaced persons.

The U.S. Departments of State and Homeland Security have taken a number of steps to improve the pace of resettlement processing for Iraqi refugees. After resettling only 202 and 1,608 Iraqi refugees in 2006 and 2007 respectively, the U.S. Refugee Admissions Program (USRAP) is now resettling significantly more Iraqis, with over 18,000 Iraqi refugees resettled to the United States in fiscal year 2009, as well as in 2010. In early 2008, the U.S. government began to set up the priority resettlement and special immigrant visa programs that were mandated by Congress in the Refugee Crisis in Iraq Act in order to bring U.S.-affiliated Iraqis to safety without delay—and has established a system for processing the resettlement requests of U.S.- affiliated Iraqis "in-country," i.e. from within Iraq.

In January 2010, the State Department doubled the grant for newly arrived refugees, which is essential to support their integration into their new homes and communities in the United States, a long-overdue increase that has provided additional assistance for many resettled Iraqi refugees who are struggling in the face of the U.S. economic downturn.[13] The State Department has also expressed commitment to review its practices and the potential for developing more formalized policy relating to emergency and urgent resettlement. The National Security Council and the State Department also began examining some of the impediments that are undermining the effectiveness of the special immigrant visa program that was designed to bring some U.S.-affiliated Iraqis to safety. In addition, the U.S. Citizenship and Immigration Service

(USCIS), part of the Department of Homeland of Security, has committed to undertaking a series of reforms to increase transparency as it adjudicates resettlement applications.[14]

Persistent Problems: Human Rights First's Primary Findings and Recommendations

Despite the progress made over the last three years, however, Human Rights First's research has documented a number of persistent delays, inefficiencies and other flaws in the processing of U.S. resettlement and special immigrant visa applications. These problems continue to impede the ability of the United States to operate its resettlement efforts in a timely and transparent manner—and undermine efforts of the United States to bring U.S.-affiliated Iraqis to safety without delay.

Human Rights First's findings include:

1. Delays in the processing of U.S. background checks leave Iraqi refugees and U.S.-affiliated Iraqis—including families and children—in difficult and dangerous situations for prolonged periods of time, undermining the commitment of the United States to protect refugees;

■ *Slow processing and a substantial backlog undermines effectiveness of priority resettlement and immigrant visa programs for U.S.-affiliated Iraqis.* The cases of more than 26,000 U.S.-affiliated Iraqis who have applied for U.S. resettlement through a priority access program which enables direct applications for U.S. resettlement— known as Priority 2 (P2) access—are "in various stages of processing," with 25,000 of those individuals still inside Iraq.[15] The current processing time for U.S.-affiliated Iraqis applying for U.S. resettlement through this program ranges from 12 to 21 months.[16] For those applying to a separate special immigrant visa program the processing time ranges from 9 to 17 months, including a six-month delay for security checks, according to

Human Rights First interviews with *pro bono* attorneys.

■ *Security clearance processing takes an average of five months for Iraqi refugees, often longer.* The conduct of effective security checks is an essential step in the screening of any individual who enters the United States. The security check process necessarily requires time and attention, including to analyze applicants who may have common names. However, the average time for conducting a security advisory opinion is five months for Iraqi refugees[17]—meaning that many Iraqis wait longer than five months for their checks to clear. Human Rights First researchers interviewed a number of refugee families in Jordan, Lebanon and Egypt who had been waiting for nine or ten months—or even longer—after other processing had been completed, for their security processing to be concluded.

■ *Delays in background checks slow pace of resettlement and visa processing for Iraqis facing danger.* Both the Government Accountability Office (GAO) and the Ombudsman of U.S. Citizenship and Immigration Services have confirmed that the waiting time for security clearances has led to extended delays in resettlement processing for some Iraqi refugees. The State Department reported to the GAO in 2009 that about 53 percent of the Iraqi refugees who had been approved for resettlement but had not yet left for the United States had not done so because the State Department was awaiting completion of security check processing from the Central Intelligence Agency (CIA), and that insufficient personnel to process clearances at the CIA had become a significant issue for many immigrant and refugee applicants, including Iraqis.[18] For U.S.-affiliated Iraqis, Human Rights First interviews confirmed that security clearance checks remain the longest step in the process, for both special immigrant visa and P2 resettlement applicants. These checks—which are initiated by the United States government early in the application process—can take up to an additional five months *after* an application has otherwise been approved, according to Human Rights First interviews with *pro bono* lawyers representing U.S.-affiliated Iraqis.

■ *Delays leave Iraqi refugees and U.S.-affiliated Iraqis and their families stranded in difficult and dangerous situations; the lack of information provided to refugees on processing times makes it difficult for them to plan their futures.* Iraqi refugee and immigrant visa applicants and their families often wait for decisions on their cases while still living in Iraq or elsewhere in the region, facing the daily threat of violence and/or serious financial challenges because they are not legally authorized to work. For example, the son of an Iraqi translator who worked for the U.S. military waited 21 months in Baghdad for his resettlement approval, suffering a shooting due to his father's U.S. affiliation as well as additional threats while waiting for the security check process to be completed; he finally arrived in the United States in November 2010.[19] In Jordan, Human Rights First was informed of an Iraqi refugee who had worked for the U.S. military and contractors for three years, and after waiting over a year for his security clearance to be completed, was now destitute and unable to support his family.[20] Delays in security checks also left children and families in dangerous situations. In one case, a family was threatened by a militia group that had targeted the family in Iraq, while while they waited for their security clearance to be completed in a third country. In another case, a child fell ill and died while awaiting security processing, and his young siblings and mother were jailed by Turkish authorities because they had overstayed their visas.[21] The lack of accurate information and misunderstandings relating to the timeframe for a resettlement decision led some refugees interviewed by Human Rights First to withdraw or withhold their children from schools, sell their belongings and quit their jobs as they mistakenly believed that their departure to the United States was imminent.

2. The special resettlement and immigrant visa programs for U.S.-affiliated Iraqis—created by Congress with broad bi-partisan support to bring to safety Iraqis who worked for the U.S. military, government, or contractors, U.S media or non-government groups, as well as religious minorities with U.S. family ties—are still hampered by inefficiencies and delays, including excessively long processing times, lengthy delays due to the security clearance process (as discussed above), and for the special immigrant visa program in particular, low application levels.

■ *Special programs remain slow and inefficient.* The programs mandated by Congress in the Refugee Crisis in Iraq Act to create escape routes for U.S.-affiliated Iraqis have been operational since 2008, but almost three years later, Human Rights First research indicates that these programs remain slow and inefficient. The programs have brought approximately 12,700 U.S.-affiliated Iraqis to safety in the United States since their inception. While this number represents a welcome improvement since 2009, when Human Rights First issued a report on the programs,[22] many more U.S.-affiliated Iraqis—26,000 as noted above—have resettlement applications that are still "in various stages of processing". Furthermore, Human Rights First has found that the processing time for applications to these programs remains quite long—one to two years, according to our interviews, including a significant wait time for the initial interview. As detailed above, and in Section III of this report, a primary reason for these delays appears to be the delays in the conduct of security processing. These lengthy processing times undermine the ability of the programs to achieve their objectives, as the long delays leave at-risk applicants exposed to further hardship and violence, especially inside Iraq, where high levels of violence persist.

■ *Lack of improvement in processing times for, and inefficiencies remain in the Special Immigrant Visa (SIV) program:* Due to the prioritization of Iraqi SIV applications by U.S. Citizenship and Immigration Services (USCIS), the processing time at one stage of the SIV process has decreased to just one to three weeks. However, overall processing times for SIV applications do not appear to have improved significantly since the inception of the SIV program. While the State Department did not provide information on total processing times in response to requests from Human Rights First, according to our interviews with *pro bono* attorneys who represent U.S.-affiliated Iraqis, the SIV process can take 9 to 17 months from start to finish.[23] A number of inefficiencies appear to have contributed to the slow processing times. In particular, the length of time that it takes for applicants to receive "Chief of Mission" (COM) approvals from the U.S. Embassy in Baghdad has increased from six to eight weeks (as reported by Human Rights First in April 2009)[24] to three to four months, according to the State Department. Other Human Rights First interviews indicate that it may take as long as six months to one year.[25] One reason for this delay relates to the contract staff who conduct document collection for the State Department and sometimes request unnecessary or inappropriate documentation from applicants. For example, Iraqis have been asked to provide copies of the contract between the U.S. government and a major U.S. contractor—a document they would have no reason to possess and can be difficult or impossible to obtain. The State Department is working to address these inefficiencies, but it is too soon to assess the impact of planned changes.

■ *Low application levels for SIV program:* The Iraqi SIV program suffers from low application levels, likely because the application process is so lengthy and complex, and often inefficient, as discussed above. Since the inception of the program and as of September 2010, the State Department had issued just 2,524 SIVs to Iraqis who worked for the U.S. government, military or contractors (plus an additional 2,523 visas to their spouses and children, who are included in the applications of the principal applicants).[26] While this represents a significant increase from March 2009, when Human Rights First reported that only 641 Iraqis had been issued SIVs,[27] the total number of SIVs issued to U.S.-affiliated Iraqis—2,524—is still only a small percentage of the 15,000 SIVs available for the first three years of the five-year program.

■ *Delays and inefficiencies undermine purpose of programs*: In explaining the need for these programs, the late Senator Edward Kennedy (D-MA) suggested before Congress that "8 to 10 months" was too long to wait for "courageous Iraqis... who have worked with the American military, the staff of our Embassy, or with American organizations to support our mission in Iraq."[28] When the programs were included in the Defense Authorization Conference Report in December 2007, prior to their adoption into law, Senator Sam Brownback (R-KS) said, "So many brave Iraqis have risked their lives and the lives of their family members to support our effort there. We thank them, we applaud them, and we will not leave them in their time of need."[29] As confirmed by the interviews and case examples included in this report, the processing delays and inefficiencies are leaving U.S.-affiliated Iraqis stranded in difficult and dangerous situations—failing the very Iraqis that these programs were meant to support.

3. The United States lacks a formal and transparent procedure for expediting the resettlement of refugees who face imminent danger and require emergency or urgent resettlement to preserve their physical security. The Department of State is working to address this gap.

■ *Effective expedited resettlement systems are needed to protect refugees facing imminent risks of harm*. Human Rights First has learned that the 700 places provided for emergency resettlement globally (by resettlement countries *other than* the United States) are typically filled by the middle of each year.[30] At the same time, UNHCR confirmed in a May 2010 paper that "acute risks faced by refugees increasingly oblige UNHCR to resort to emergency resettlement," leading it to recommend that States strengthen or establish emergency resettlement systems.[31] Through our research on the resettlement of Iraqi refugees, Human Rights First collected a number of examples of Iraqi refugees whose situations illustrate the broader need for an effective expedited resettlement procedure on behalf of the United States. For example, in Jordan, Human Rights First interviewed an Iraqi refugee family with a three-year-old daughter who was very ill. The child was suffering from severe kidney disease and required medical treatment that was not available in Jordan to save her life. Although UNHCR wanted to refer the family for resettlement, there was a shortage of resettlement places for urgent medical cases, and the case was not referred to the United States due to the unpredictability of U.S. processing times. Human Rights First also learned of several cases of Iraqi women who were in danger in Syria and Jordan because male family members were actively searching for them in order to inflict harm, as well as the case of a gay Iraqi man who had fled to a country within the region only to have his life threatened there because of his sexual orientation.[32]

■ *Lack of transparent U.S. expedited procedure limits options for refugees who face imminent danger; United States examines potential of developing an expedited resettlement procedure.* While the United States does expedite individual refugee cases,[33] the lack of an actual procedure hinders the ability of refugees in need of expedited resettlement to find safety. Due to the lack of a formal process, local UNHCR offices and non-governmental organizations that assist refugees have no way of knowing how to refer a refugee for expedited U.S. resettlement or what the criteria are for such an expedited resettlement. The State Department's overseas resettlement processing entities (OPEs) also lack consistent and clear guidance. In a set of recommendations issued in 2009, the Ombudsman for U.S. Citizenship and Immigration Services (USCIS) found a lack of transparency in the procedure for requesting expedited resettlement in emergent cases and recommended that USCIS publicly state the criteria for expediting emergent refugee cases and how to access that expedited process.[34] In response, USCIS is working in partnership with the Department of State to develop information on how to request an expedited process for a pending refugee case.[35]

■ *Inability of U.S. government to provide a firm timeline for processing, including security processing, undermines its capacity to create a transparent emergency resettlement procedure.* The capacity of the United States to expedite refugee cases is hampered by the inability of the U.S. resettlement program to provide firm timelines for processing, and in particular for the completion of security processing. The Department of State has informed non-governmental groups that its total estimated expedited processing time ranges from two weeks to five months—a fairly wide range of time.[36] While two weeks may assist a refugee who is facing imminent danger, five months is too slow to ensure the protection of a refugee who faces life-threatening risks. As David Martin pointed out in a 2005 report commissioned by the State Department, the Departments of State and Homeland Security "should work together to restore the capacity to act *in a matter of days or weeks* to approve and resettle refugee persons who are in grave and immediate danger and whose cases are referred by UNHCR or a U.S. Embassy..... Such cases will be exceptional and

the volume of such cases can be expected to be quite low, thus making special arrangements feasible."[37] In its July 2010 response to the Ombudsman's recommendation on expedited resettlement, USCIS asserted that both it and the Department of State lacked the ability to ensure that security checks conducted by other government agencies were completed within a certain time frame.[38]

4. A lack of basic information—essential to ensuring transparency and fairness in resettlement decision-making—undermines the effectiveness and purpose of U.S. resettlement program and its Request for Reconsideration process.

■ *Lack of information on denial letters undermine ability to request reconsideration of decisions.* When a refugee is determined to be ineligible for U.S. resettlement, she or he is only provided with general reasons for the denial, a level of information that makes it difficult to impossible for the refugee to submit a meaningful request for review. While USCIS revised its denial letters (known as "Notices of Ineligibility") in 2009, the revisions still leave refugees with only general explanations for their denials. Indeed the USCIS Ombudsman's Office has recommended that USCIS "articulate .. clear and *case-specific* information regarding the grounds for denial."[39] Human Rights First has reviewed numerous denial letters that provide inadequate information. For example, one Iraqi woman who fled after her family had been threatened due to her husband's work on a U.S. military base and after she herself had been seriously injured was told only that her resettlement request was denied because of a "lack of credibility."[40] Another Iraqi, who had worked for U.S. contractors in Iraq for years and been threatened with harm repeatedly by militia groups, was told only that his application for U.S. resettlement was denied "for other reasons."[41] When Human Rights First researchers asked him if he was going to submit a Request for Reconsideration, he pondered, "What would I put in my appeal, even if I were to file it?"[42]

■ *Lack of information hampers representation by legal counsel.* While the availability of legal counsel to assist refugees with resettlement is extremely scarce, there are a few *pro bono* attorneys who help U.S-affiliated Iraqis, as well as a small number of non-profit projects that provide legal counsel refugees around the world who are pursuing resettlement. But since the United States does not permit legal counsel from attending resettlement interviews, and provides insufficient information about the reasons for denials, even these few legal representatives are often left without the information they need to submit effective Requests for Reconsideration. Instead, these attorneys—and their refugee clients—are left to speculate about the potential basis for the decision.

■ *Critical information written only in English.* Many refugees moreover do not know that they can request a review and do not understand the limited information that is provided to them as it is written only in English. While USCIS has agreed to develop standardized information explaining how refugees can request a review,[43] this information will need to be translated into the languages that refugees understand in order to be effective. The denial letter itself—which informs refugees that they can request a review—is written only in English.

To address the problems identified in this report, Human Rights First has outlined a comprehensive set of recommended reforms—for the U.S. government, UNHCR, refugee-hosting governments and the Iraqi government. These recommendations follow this summary, and additional recommendations on the post-arrival needs of Iraqi refugees in the United States are included in Appendix II to this report.

Our primary recommendations to the U.S. government include:

Ensure timely and effective processing of refugee resettlement and visa applications for Iraqis, including U.S.-affiliated Iraqis and other refugees—specifically:

■ **Reduce unnecessary delays in the security clearance process.** The **National Security Council** should, together with the Departments of State, Justice, Homeland Security and intelligence agencies, improve the inter-agency security clearance procedure to enable security checks for refugees and U.S.-affiliated Iraqis to be completed accurately and without unnecessary delays within a set time period. Focal points should also be established within each agency to ensure that each case moves through the clearance process in a timely manner, and the necessary staffing and prioritization should be provided. These improvements will serve to enhance the effectiveness of the security clearance process more broadly;

■ **Develop and implement an emergency resettlement procedure for refugees facing imminent danger.** The **Department of State** should continue to work with other relevant federal agencies to develop and implement a formal and transparent resettlement procedure for refugees who face emergency or urgent circumstances—which most importantly includes a set timeframe for processing emergency and urgent cases;

■ **Remove other impediments which continue to delay the applications of U.S.-affiliated Iraqis.** The **Department of State**, working with other agencies, should—in addition to addressing delays in security processing—continue to take other steps to eliminate P2 and SIV case backlogs and address inefficiencies in the current SIV visa processing procedures, such as eliminating redundant or unnecessary requests for documentation at the "Chief of Mission" approval stage, establishing focal points who are authorized to track—and intervene on—SIV applications as they move throughout this complex inter-agency process, and establishing a formal review process of denials of COM approvals as well as the visa themselves; and

■ **Provide information necessary for refugees to submit meaningful Requests for Reconsideration. The Department of Homeland Security's U.S. Citizenship and Immigration Services** should implement reforms to improve the fairness and effectiveness of the resettlement process, including by revising the current Notice of Ineligibility for Resettlement to provide case-specific factual and legal reasons for denial, ensuring that the Notice is written in a language a refugee can understand. and move ahead with its commitment to provide information on the process for requesting review— which should also be provided in the appropriate languages.

The findings and recommendations contained in this report are based on interviews with Iraqi refugees; interviews and meetings with officials of various governments, including the U.S. government; interviews and correspondence with staff of UNHCR and civil society organizations; and interviews and correspondence with *pro bono* attorneys who represent U.S.-affiliated Iraqis. Human Rights First also requested information from the U.S. government and from UNHCR. Human Rights First researchers conducted approximately fifty interviews with Iraqi refugees and other research between April and November 2010 in Jordan. Lebanon, Egypt and the United States. The Syrian government did not grant visas to Human Rights First researchers, so we were unable to interview Iraqi refugees and others in Syria. We did, however, interview Iraqis who currently live in the United States who had initially sought refuge in Syria.

Through addressing the inefficiencies and other problems in Iraqi resettlement processing, the United States would improve the effectiveness of its resettlement program for all refugees—and would strengthen its leadership role as a model for global resettlement programming more broadly. Moreover, resettlement can help to maintain and expand protection within refugee-hosting states by demonstrating a commitment to share in the responsibility for addressing the plight of men, women and children who have been forced to flee their home in search of safe refuge.

Recommendations

To the President:

■ **Strengthened engagement on Iraqi displacement**: Retain and strengthen the role of the White House Senior Coordinator on Iraqi Refugees and Internally Displaced Persons (IDPs) to ensure continued inter-agency cooperation, planning and improvements regarding all stages of Iraqi displacement, including resettlement, local integration and voluntary return and reintegration, as well as in the specialized programs established to resettle Iraqis who face persecution on account of their work with the United States. Ensure the Coordinator continues to convene regular meetings with federals agencies and civil society groups, as well as conducts missions to both the region and Iraq itself;

■ **Enable security checks to be completed accurately and without unnecessary delays**: Together with the Departments of State, Justice, Homeland Security and intelligence agencies, improve the inter-agency security clearance procedure for refugees and immigrants through ensuring adequate staffing, coordination and/or prioritization to enable clearance checks to be completed accurately and without unnecessary delays within a set time period; establish focal points within each agency to ensure that each case moves through the clearance process in a timely manner;

■ **Provide necessary leadership to ensure the development and implementation of an emergency resettlement procedure**: Provide oversight and ensure cooperation of relevant federal agencies to develop a formalized and transparent emergency resettlement procedure which allows resettlement processing to be completed within a set time period for refugees who face urgent or emergency circumstances;

■ **Continue White House review of U.S. resettlement program**: Continue the comprehensive review of the U.S. resettlement program and ensure that the challenges detailed in this report are addressed in that review;

■ **Support protection of Iraqi refugees in the Middle East region**: Encourage and support host governments in the region to strengthen protection of refugees in the region, including by providing continued humanitarian assistance for Iraqi refugees, promoting access to formal employment, and urging that national authorities not detain Iraqi refugees solely on account of their "illegal" presence;

■ **Encourage strengthened Iraqi government responsibility to provide solutions for displaced persons**: Urge the Government of Iraq to take concrete steps to improve the situation of returnees and displaced persons inside Iraq; such steps should include developing a work plan to address the needs of Iraqi IDPs and returnees, implementing effective mechanisms to promote sustainable reintegration, ensuring that the Iraqi legal framework on displacement complies with international human rights standards, and taking other steps to ensure the protection of returning refugees and IDPs.

To the Department of State:

■ **Decrease processing times for specialized U.S.-affiliated resettlement programs**: Take steps to reduce the significant backlog of Priority 2 (P2) applications, especially inside Iraq, and decrease current processing times for resettlement applications, which currently amount to one to two years;

■ **Reduce barriers to the special immigrant visa (SIV) program for U.S.-affiliated Iraqis**: Address inefficiencies in the current SIV processing procedures, including redundant or unnecessary requests for documentation at the "Chief of Mission" (COM) approval stage, establish focal points to track SIV applications, and establish a formal review process of denials of COM approvals as well as the visa themselves;

■ **Develop and implement a formalized emergency resettlement procedure**: In collaboration with relevant federal agencies and civil society groups, establish a formal and transparent resettlement procedure for refugees who face emergency or urgent circumstances, which includes the following elements:

  • A list of criteria or indicators to determine whether a case should be expedited;

  • Identification of the steps that must be expedited, which may depend on location and referral source but include: UNHCR registration and refugee determination, OPE procedures, DHS interview(s), sponsorship assurance, pre-departure preparations and security clearances;

  • A set timeframe for processing expedited cases, which should not be longer than seven days for emergency cases. If the Department of State cannot ensure processing within this timeframe, measures should be taken to ensure the protection of the refugee, including (with the refugee's consent) through relocation to one of UNHCR's

Evacuation Transfer Facilities pursuant to its processing procedures and guidelines.

■ **Review partner agency emergency resettlement procedures**: Conduct a review of the emergency resettlement procedures utilized by the Department's resettlement partner agencies—known as Overseas Processing Entities (OPEs)—to ensure they conform to the Department's own procedures and processes;

■ **Provide consistent information to refugees whose resettlement applications are on hold or delayed**: Ensure that OPEs provide standard guidance to refugees whose applications are on hold—or "deferred"—because of security checks or other reasons. Work with USCIS to revise letters to refugees who are deferred to include additional information (a recommendation on this letter is included below);

■ **Ensure the principle of family unity when cases are delayed:** When resettlement approvals for one or more family members are delayed to clearance delays, take steps to request more expedited processing of the clearance so that the family is not separated or forced, due to the difficulty of their circumstances, to proceed with U.S. resettlement while still not knowing if the remaining family member/s will be able to join them;

■ **Support UNHCR's Evacuation Transfer Facilities:** Continue to financially support UNHCR's Evacuation Transfer Facilities to be used as a means to protect refugees who face life-threatening situations, as well as UNHCR's ability to identify emergency and urgent cases that require expedited processing;

■ **Demonstrate leadership in funding the U.N.'s Iraq appeals**: Continue to lead the international community in responding to current and future U.N. Iraq and Iraqi refugee appeals at no less than 50 percent; continue to encourage other donor States to make contributions;

■ **Continue resettlement of Iraqi refugees and increase the pace**: Continue resettlement of Iraqi refugees at existing levels at least; increase the pace of processing to allow those applicants who are approved to depart without unnecessary delays.

To the Department of Homeland Security's U.S. Citizenship and Immigration Services:

■ **Provide standardized guidance to refugees who may be resettled to the United States, including those whose cases are delayed or "deferred"**: Revise the current letter issued to all refugees whose requests for resettlement are "deferred." The letter—which should be translated into local languages—should include the following elements:

- Information to ensure that refugees understand that they have not been accepted for U.S. resettlement;

- A timeframe for a decision, even if approximate;

- Clear instructions which inform refugees that they should carefully considering taking any action—such as selling their possessions or withdrawing children from school—until they receive a formal acceptance;

■ **Provide specific reasons to refugees who are denied resettlement**: Revise the current Notice of Ineligibility for Resettlement to include the factual and legal reasons for denial. Such information should provide specific reasons for denial that would enable applicants to submit meaningful Requests for Reconsideration. If a denial is based on credibility, the Notice of Ineligibility should include the specific basis for the denial, such as what portions of the testimony were found not credible. The Notice of Ineligibility should also be translated into local languages;

■ **Ensure refugees understand how to submit Requests for Reconsideration**. Issue guidance on how to file a Request for Reconsideration (RFR), which includes information on where and how to submit RFRs. Guidance should also include an explanation of the process, identify the types of information and/or supporting documents that may be appropriate to submit as part of an RFR, and confirm that submission of RFRs will be acknowledged in writing;

■ **Ensure refugees can actually understand information provided**. Translate all RFR-related guidance and the Notice of Ineligibility into local languages.

To Congress:

■ **Continue to provide oversight on U.S. response to needs of Iraqi refugees**. Continue to monitor the situation of Iraqi refugees and provide funds that allow Iraqi refugees and displaced persons to meet their basic needs.

■ **Ensure processing without delays**. Provide oversight to the Departments of State, Homeland Security and intelligence agencies to ensure they work together to reduce processing times for all applications, including P2 resettlement and SIV applications from U.S.-affiliated Iraqis—which are currently a year or more for programs designed to facilitate an escape to safety for its applicants;

■ **Ensure funds are available to implement an emergency resettlement procedure**. Fund as appropriate the Department of State to establish a formal and transparent resettlement procedure for refugees who face emergency circumstances.

To the U.N. Refugee Agency—UNHCR:

- **Inform refugees if they are not going to be resettled**. Consistently inform refugees if they are not going to be referred for resettlement. If there are instances where it remains uncertain if a particular case will or will not be referred, UNHCR should provide refugees with a range of time in which it expects a final decision;

- **Ensure exclusion processes comply with fairness standards**. Review exclusion identification decision-making processes and procedures to ensure they conform to procedural fairness standards;

- **Issue guidance on use of Emergency Transit Facilities**. Develop information for NGOs and UNHCR field offices on how and under what circumstances requests can be made to evacuate refugees to a UNHCR Emergency Transit Facility;

- **Decrease time required for evacuations to Emergency Transit Facilities**. Continue to explore practical ways to decrease processing time required for evacuations to Emergency Transit Facilities to 14 days or less;

- **Ensure Emergency Transit Facilities are able to support all refugees**. Review and ensure that Emergency Transit Facilities are able to address the needs of all refugees, including, for example, single women, LGBTI refugees and survivors of torture;

- **Increase capacity to identify and process emergency and urgent resettlement cases**. Strengthen capacity to identify and process refugees who require emergency or urgent resettlement in collaboration with resettlement NGOs.

To Refugee-Hosting Countries, Including Jordan, Syria, Lebanon, Turkey and Egypt:

- **Facilitate resettlement**. Continue to take steps to facilitate the resettlement of Iraqi refugees, including by waiving exit fees and providing visas to U.S. refugee officers to conduct resettlement interviews in a timely manner;

- **Enable refugees to formalize their legal status and work legally**. Grant refugees at least temporary legal status and ensure their access to formal employment;

- **Do not detain or deport Iraqi refugees solely because of their illegal status**. Instruct security agencies and police to not detain Iraqi refugees or asylum seekers solely on the basis of their illegal presence in the country;

- **Ratify the 1951 Convention**. Syria, Lebanon, and Jordan should ratify the 1951 Convention Relating to the Status of Refugees, and all countries should develop specific legal frameworks which define and protect the rights of refugees;

- **Allow refugees to access services**. Enable refugees to access services, such as education and social support, on par with nationals;

- **Cooperate with UNHCR and NGOs**. Continue to cooperate with UNHCR and non-governmental organizations to increase and expand refugee protection.

To the Government of Iraq:

■ **Take concrete steps to ensure the protection of refugees who choose to return voluntarily as well as Iraqi IDPs, including by increasing returnee stipends and developing a work plan to address IDP needs**. Provide support to refugee-hosting countries including Syria and Jordan, to ensure the protection of Iraqi refugees in those countries. The Iraqi government should also provide additional resources to increase the capacity of Iraq's Ministry of Displacment and Migration, ensure that newly displaced Iraqis are able to register for assistance and protection—and develop assistance and support for those IDPs who wish to remain in their place of displacement as well as return.

I. Protection of Iraqi Refugees in the Region since 2003

Since the start of the war in Iraq in March 2003, and particularly since the outbreak of sectarian violence in February 2006 following the Samarra Mosque bombing, more than 2 million Iraqis have fled their homes. Approximately 1.5 million people remain internally displaced within Iraq following the violence in 2006,[44] and hundreds of thousands of Iraqis have sought refuge in other countries in the region. As of October 2010, 195,428 Iraqi refugees are registered with the U.N. Refugee Agency, UNHCR, in Egypt, Iran, Jordan, Lebanon, Syria, Turkey and the Gulf Cooperation Council States, with the majority located in Jordan and Syria.[45] An unknown number of Iraqi refugees have not registered with UNHCR. As their months and years of exile increase, with no end in sight, the vulnerabilities and needs of these displaced Iraqis continue to rise.

In light of ongoing insecurity and violence, and highly limited access to basic services, Iraqis continue to flee their country, and the number of Iraqi refugees returning home is low. Between January and October 2010, over 31,000 Iraqi refugees registered for the first time with UNHCR in the region, including over 3,000 new registrations in Syria and Jordan in the month of October.[46] Very few Iraqi refugees repatriated voluntarily with UNHCR assistance; from January to October 2010, only 520 individuals had requested UNHCR support to return.[47] Many more Iraqi refugees—some 22,000 over the same period—returned without UNHCR assistance.[48] Yet even this figure represents a small percentage of the total displaced population. UNHCR has reaffirmed that "the basic conditions necessary to encourage and sustain large scale return to Iraq have not yet been established."[49] A UNHCR survey released in October 2010 also found that a majority of Iraqis who had returned to Baghdad regretted their decision to return due to physical insecurity, economic hardship and inadequate access to basic services.[50] Upon return, these Iraqis experienced

high levels of violence. These returnees explained that they had returned because they could no longer afford the high cost of living in neighboring refugee-hosting states such as Syria and Jordan.[51]

Human Rights First interviews in the region with Iraqi refugees confirm that many believe it is not safe to return due to the continued violence and insecurity, limited access to services and uncertainty about Iraq's future. Indeed, the severe difficulties and prolonged delays in government formation are primary indicators of the uncertainty about Iraq's political future and stability. Along these lines, one refugee in Amman stated, "Things will most certainly get worse in Iraq since the elections. How can I expose my family to that violence again?"[52] Another Iraqi refugee said, "The situation is even worse now; the elections are meaningless. Iran is ruling Iraq, not the Iraqi government."[53]

Challenges of Local Integration

Iraqis who flee Iraq continue to seek refuge primarily in the region, with the majority of Iraqi refugees now living in Syria and Jordan. Others have fled to Lebanon, Turkey and Egypt and as well other states. Refugee-hosting countries, including Syria and Jordan, which host the bulk of refugees from Iraq, have generally received Iraqis in their countries and allowed them to live among their populations. Yet the ability of Iraqi refugees to integrate locally on a long-term basis in the region—for example, to work legally, to obtain a secure legal status, and to enjoy other basic rights–is highly limited due to a number of serious obstacles.

Syria, Jordan and Lebanon—where the majority of Iraqi refugees live—are not parties to the 1951 U.N. Convention Relating to the Status of Refugees or its 1967 Protocol. The 1951 Refugee Convention sets forth the legal definition of a refugee and enumerates the rights of refugees. These countries do not have legal frameworks through which refugees can access their rights, and they lack domestic refugee or asylum legislation.[54] When Human Rights First researchers met with Jordanian and Lebanese government officials, these officials did not use the term "refugees" to refer to the Iraqis residing in their countries, but referred to them as "temporary guests."[55] Although Egypt is a signatory to both the 1951 Convention and its 1967 Protocol, it has made several reservations to the Convention[56] and also lacks domestic asylum legislation.

The political environment in these host countries also presents challenges to refugee integration. Some governments in the region have argued that their capacity to absorb Iraqi refugees is limited because of their large existing Palestinian refugee populations.[57] In addition, Egyptian authorities, who have long perceived the Shi'a sect as a threat that must be contained,[58] continue to view Iraqi refugees who are Shi'a with a great deal of suspicion.[59]

Limited Access to Employment and Services

Throughout the region, refugees are not authorized to work based on their status as "refugees." Indeed, many of these states do not even recognize the status of "refugee" in their own domestic legal frameworks. Instead, refugees have—at most—only the same right to work as other foreigners, meaning that they need to be "sponsored" by nationals of the host country—a process that is both lengthy and expensive. Furthermore, high unemployment rates in the region effectively preclude most refugees from access to the formal labor market. As a result, most are thrust into the informal labor market, where refugees can only work illegally, exposing them to the constant risk of arrest, detention and possible deportation, as well as various kinds of exploitation.

In Amman, Human Rights First researchers met an Iraqi Mandean family who had fled Iraq in 2004. Four years later, in 2008, the family was struggling financially. Shortly after the eldest son found a job in a restaurant to help support his struggling family, he was arrested for working illegally.[60] He was detained for three days in a

Jordanian jail before his family could gather the bail money to secure his release. "Now he doesn't even leave the house," his mother said.[61] In Abu Alanda, a neighborhood on the outskirts of Amman, Human Rights First researchers interviewed a young Iraqi man who reported that he had been detained for six weeks because he was working illegally in a bakery to support his family.[62]

Iraqi refugees also struggle to locate and pay for housing—an enormous challenge for refugees without access to legal work. One Iraqi refugee in Egypt said, "Every time I am even a little bit late with the rent, my landlord says he will report me to the police."[63] Lawyers at a legal aid organization in Amman also reported to Human Rights First that their attorneys routinely handle problems Iraqis face with landlords.[64] While UNHCR provides direct financial assistance to vulnerable refugees, which for example, assisted some 4,000 Iraqi refugee families in Jordan as of May 2010, due to budgetary reasons the number of families receiving cash assistance is limited.[65]

Many Iraqi refugees and their families lack adequate access to education and health care. Iraqi children are able to attend public schools in Lebanon, Jordan, and Syria. This access has been facilitated by the significant amounts of assistance provided by the international community—including the United States—to support education for Iraqi children in the region.[66] But in Egypt, Iraqi children are not permitted to attend national schools and instead children are left without schooling unless their parents can earn or find the money to send their children to private schools.[67] As the refugee situation becomes increasingly protracted, it is unclear how long the governments of Lebanon, Jordan and Syria will continue to support the education of Iraqi children—particularly if international aid for the education of Iraqi children should decline.[68] Funding shortfalls have already forced UNHCR to cut assistance programs for some of the most vulnerable Iraqi refugees, including for tertiary health care.[69] This lack of health care is of particular concern given the well-documented medical needs and traumatic experiences suffered by many Iraqi refugees.[70]

Detention and Other Protection Concerns

Iraqi refugees face a number of difficulties which threaten their safety and physical security. In Lebanon, prolonged detention and forced return remain a serious concern. At the end of October 2010, more than 90 asylum seekers and refugees remained in detention in Lebanon, the majority of whom were Iraqi.[71] In most cases detention of refugees and asylum seekers is due to what Lebanese authorities deem as "illegal entry or stay" or due to minor offenses such as violation of labor regulations.[72] In October, at least eight Iraqi persons of concern to UNHCR were deported from Lebanon.[73] In Syria, as of December 2010 there were approximately 100 detained Iraqi refugees, and it is likely that there are additional cases that UNHCR is not aware of.[74] In Jordan, UNHCR informed Human Rights First that its staff intervenes on an average of 10 cases of detained Iraqis per month.[75] While these numbers are relatively small, the risk of detention causes Iraqi and other refugees to remain underground. An Iraqi refugee in Amman told Human Rights First researchers, "Our savings from Baghdad are finishing. We don't experience harassment but we are trying to keep a low profile so we don't get into trouble."[76]

In addition to detention, refugees face additional protection challenges, including the threat of sexual and gender-based violence. In Jordan, Human Rights First researchers interviewed a divorced Iraqi woman who lived alone with her 10-year-old son and reported that she was being stalked by a Jordanian man who had physically abused her and threatened, on more than one occasion, to have her deported.[77] Social workers in Jordan have also expressed concern about the increase in domestic violence among refugee families which has been exacerbated by the increasing strain and pressures of exile, in addition to many refugees' own past experiences of trauma in Iraq.[78] Iraqis who have fled persecution on account of their sexual orientation or gender identity also face a particular set of vulnerabilities as countries in the region including Syria and Lebanon, criminalize same-sex behavior or target LGBTI people.[79]

Resettlement As a Durable Solution

UNHCR has stated that "local integration is not possible for the vast majority of Iraqi refugees."[80] Indeed, given the many challenges outlined above, neither local integration in the region nor return to Iraq are viable options for the vast majority of Iraq's refugees. For this reason, resettlement to third countries will remain a vital tool for providing protection as well as long-term durable solutions to Iraqi refugees which allow them to rebuild their lives in safety and with dignity.

Currently UNHCR plays the primary role in identifying refugees who are in need of resettlement. Once refugees register with UNHCR, its staff will determine the degree to which Iraqi and other refugees meet one or more of its resettlement eligibility criteria.[81] If UNHCR concludes that a refugee is eligible for resettlement, the agency submits a resettlement registration form to one of the resettlement countries—commonly known as a resettlement referral. Once UNHCR submits a referral, the refugee must undergo the processing required by the particular resettlement country.

In the case of a resettlement referral to the United States, the Department of State's U.S. Refugee Admissions Program (USRAP) contracts with individual Overseas Processing Entities (OPEs) to manage and facilitate refugee resettlement overseas. In Jordan, Syria and Egypt the OPE is the International Organization of Migration (IOM), and in Lebanon and Turkey the International Catholic Migration Commission (ICMC) acts as the OPE. The OPEs are the interface among the Department of State, the Department of Homeland Security and the refugee applicant. Once a refugee is referred by UNHCR for resettlement, the OPE coordinates a multi-stage and multi-agency application process that includes medical and security checks, as well as adjudication interviews conducted by specially trained officers from the U.S. Citizenship and Immigration Services (USCIS), an agency that is part of the Department of Homeland Security. These officers conduct ongoing "circuit rides" to the region to interview refugee applicants. As the USRAP acknowledges, "resettlement to the United States is a long process that can take months, or even years."[82]

While most Iraqi refugees require a referral from UNHCR in order to be resettled to the United States, several groups of Iraqis—primarily those who worked for the U.S. government or other U.S. entities—can apply for resettlement to the United States without a UNHCR referral if they live in Iraq, Jordan or Egypt; other U.S.-affiliated Iraqis can apply for special immigrant visas to the United States. The Refugee Crisis in Iraq Act, signed into law by President Bush in February 2008, created these programs to facilitate processing of U.S.-affiliated Iraqis to ensure they are able to find safety as quickly as possible. Yet as detailed in Sections II and III of this report, these programs have been hampered by extended processing delays.

UNHCR recently announced that it has referred 100,000 Iraqi refugees for resettlement since 2007,[83] the majority of whom were referred to the United States. After

resettling only 202 and 1,608 Iraqi refugees in 2006 and 2007 respectively, the USRAP is now providing durable solutions to a significantly increased number of Iraqi refugees—resettling over 18,000 refugees in fiscal year 2010.[84] Since fiscal year 2007, some 55,000 Iraqi refugees have been resettled to the United States.[85] The United States has also taken some steps over the years to improve delays in resettlement processing, and has expressed a commitment to develop expedited processing guidelines for refugees who face imminent danger.

Despite a number of improvements in the pace of U.S. resettlement processing, only 50 percent of refugees referred for resettlement by UNHCR since 2007 have actually departed.[86] While in Syria to mark World Refugee Day in June 2010, the U.N. High Commissioner for Refugees, António Guterres, specifically stated, "I call on [resettlement] countries to facilitate the speedy departure of [Iraqi] refugees they have accepted for resettlement."[87]

II. Delayed Clearance Procedures and the Impact on Refugee Protection

"The major bottlenecks are the time it takes for Security Advisory Opinion (SAO) processing... We would suggest creating a priority track for all required clearance checks for Iraqi refugees, with a goal of lowering the waiting time to 15 days."

—Former U.S. Ambassador to Iraq Ryan Crocker, September 2007, in a cable to Washington from Baghdad[88]

The conduct of effective security clearance checks is an essential step in the screening of refugees and other immigrants who enter the United States. However, as detailed in this report, the current security clearance process is plagued by delays. These delays in turn lead to inefficiencies and lengthy delays in both the refugee resettlement and the Special Immigrant Visa (SIV) programs, leaving some Iraqi refugees languishing for months and sometimes years in difficult or dangerous conditions and undermining the U.S. commitment to protect refugees. The delays in security check processing also weaken the capacity of the United States to resettle refugees who require emergency resettlement because they face imminent threats to their physical security. (The need for effective U.S. mechanisms to address the protection of refugees who face imminent risks of harm is discussed in detail in Section IV of this report.)

As detailed below, both the Government Accountability Office and the USCIS Ombudsman's Office have confirmed that the waiting time for security clearances has led to extended delays in resettlement processing for some Iraqi refugees. U.S. government officials informed civil society groups in July and September 2010 that they had previously taken some steps to improve security check processing times through devoting additional resources to the process.[89] The State Department has also

reported that it has worked with "other agencies to improve the security clearance process," and that its employees "continually monitor" the security check process "to ensure that the checks are completed in the most expeditious manner possible."[90] However, significant delays and inefficiencies remain, and hence the U.S. government will need to take additional steps to ensure an effective security clearance process that operates in a timely manner and without unnecessary delays.

Resettlement of U.S.-Affiliated and Other Iraqis Delayed Due to Security Checks

Despite the creation of special processing mechanisms for Iraqis who face persecution because of their U.S. ties, Iraqis who worked with the U.S. government, military, contractors or other U.S. entities continue to face significant delays in the processing of their resettlement and visa applications due to delays in security checks. According to Human Rights First interviews with *pro bono* attorneys representing U.S.-affiliated Iraqis, security clearance checks remain the longest step in the process for both special immigrant visa (SIV) and P2 resettlement applicants—taking up to six months after an application has otherwise been approved.

Extended waiting periods can leave Iraqi refugees in difficult situations, as they are often not permitted by host states in the region to work legally to support their families, leaving them vulnerable to exploitation and without adequate resources to provide for their families. Those who are left stranded inside Iraq can also face the constant threat of potential violence. The following case examples illustrate the challenges that Iraqi refugees face due to the delays in security clearance processing:

■ **Ahmed,**[91] **the son of an Iraqi translator who had worked for the U.S. military, waited 21 months in Baghdad for his resettlement approval, suffering a shooting and other threats due to his father's U.S. work while waiting for his security check to clear.**[92] In December 2008, Ahmed applied for refugee resettlement to the United States through the P2 priority program in Baghdad. (His father had successfully applied for a special immigrant visa due to his work for the U.S. military, but as Ahmed turned 21 just two weeks before his father applied, he became ineligible for inclusion in his father's application and had to seek protection through the refugee resettlement program.)[93] In October 2009, ten months after submitting his request for resettlement, Ahmed was shot in the shoulder due to his father's affiliation with the United States. Ahmed's attorney requested that his application be expedited, and Ahmed was soon interviewed for resettlement by USCIS in November 2009 in Baghdad. In December 2009, USCIS informed Ahmed that his security clearance was pending. In April 2010, 17 months after applying for resettlement and 6 months after his USCIS interview, Ahmed received a direct threat that he would be harmed. Yet his security clearance was still pending. His attorney again requested that his application for resettlement be expedited. In September 2010, 21 months after he had first applied for P2 priority resettlement, Ahmed's security check finally cleared, and he received approval to travel to the United States. Once Ahmed received final approval, his mother—who had stayed with him in Iraq while her husband and younger children had already traveled to the United States—had to re-interview for her special immigrant visa as so much time had elapsed which caused her visa to expire. Ahmed and his mother finally traveled to the United States in November.

■ **Samir, a translator who worked for the U.S. military and U.S. contractors in Iraq for three years, has been waiting 17 months in Jordan for his resettlement request to be processed, after receiving notice that his security clearance was still "pending" over 13 months ago.**[94] For three years, Samir worked as a translator for the U.S. military and contractors in Iraq. After being targeted because of his work for the United States, Samir fled from Iraq to Jordan along with his wife and daughters. In June 2009, he applied for P2 access to the U.S. resettlement program, and was interviewed by USCIS in July 2009. Four months later, in September 2009, Samir received notification that his security clearance was pending. More than one year after receiving this notice, and nearly a year and a half after applying for U.S. resettlement, he has still not received a final decision on his application as his security clearance is still pending. Samir has waited more than a year for his security clearance to be completed. In Jordan he lacks funds to support his family, his children are not in school, and his family is now destitute. The severe financial hardship faced by Samir and his family has caused them tremendous emotional strain.

■ **Yusuf and his family, after fleeing danger in Iraq due to their status as religious minorities and due to Yusuf's work with a U.S. company in Iraq, spent four years in Syria and Jordan waiting for resettlement to the United States, including nine months waiting for security clearances.**[95] Yusuf had been threatened in Iraq because of his work with a U.S. company, and his sister had been kidnapped because of her religion. The family is Mandean, a small Iraqi religious minority whose members have faced targeted threats, extortion, violence and murders.[96] Yusuf and his family—which includes his wife, four children and his parents—first fled to Syria in December 2006. In April 2009 IOM requested that the family travel from Syria to Jordan to facilitate their resettlement.[97] In Jordan, the family then applied for P2 access to the U.S. resettlement program. Soon after their arrival in Jordan they were interviewed by USCIS Refugee Officers, and in June 2009 they underwent medical checks. When Human Rights First researchers interviewed Yusuf in April 2010, he explained that he believed that the family's processing was complete, except that they had been waiting over nine months for his elderly parents' security checks to clear. The family believed the delay was due to the grandparents' security checks because the parents and children, and not the grandparents, had already undergone cultural orientation, which is usually the last stage of U.S. resettlement processing before departure. Upon interviewing the family, it was also clear to Human Rights First that both of the grandparents had visible medical conditions. Yusuf described the situation of his family to Human Rights First:

"We are waiting for security clearance for grandfather, and his medical concern is urgent. He has no hope because he is still waiting... [The] security clearance made us stay in this situation for nine months. We were forced to travel from country to country, and we've lost everything. We are waiting four years and two months... We are running against time for my father and mother. I can't leave them."[98]

This family also kept their children out of school as they assumed they would be departing soon after their arrival in Jordan—yet since their medical checks in June 2009 they had been awaiting a final decision on their resettlement applications.

Delays Leave Families in Dangerous Situations

Human Rights First also secured *pro bono* representation for two Iraqi men who, after being granted asylum in the United States, filed requests for their families to join them. These requests were delayed due to security checks:

■ **Family members experience imprisonment and a child dies due to illness while family is waiting for security check to clear in Turkey.** A woman and her very young children were left stranded in Turkey for over eight months after a U.S. government interview due to delays in security clearances. The family was trying to join their husband and father, who had been granted asylum in the United States after being targeted in Iraq due to his work with Coalition forces. He had immediately filed requests for his wife and children to join him here, which had been approved on an expedited basis by U.S. Citizenship and Immigration Services due to the threats to the family's safety in Iraq. The family then applied for U.S. visas in Turkey. But after an interview with the U.S. embassy, the cases disappeared into what the State Department referred to as "administrative processing." Embassy staff informed the father and his lawyers that "this is a multi-agency process we have no control over it and therefore we are not able to estimate how long it may take." During this time, one of the children became extremely ill and died. Turkish police then arrested the mother and several of the young children because their Turkish visas had expired while they were waiting. While his wife and children were in a Turkish jail, the father was informed that security clearances for his wife—a young woman who had been a housewife all her adult life—and her young children had at last come through. Mother and children were held in Turkish custody until they departed for the United States.

■ **Security clearance of 12-year-old son delays entire family's application to join their father in the United States, while family experiences ongoing threats due to the father's high-profile work with Coalition families in Iraq.** The wife and five children of an Iraqi man granted asylum in the United States were stranded for months in a third country because security clearances had not come through for one of the children, a 12-year-old boy. The family faced threats to their security not only in Iraq but also in the country where they were awaiting visa processing, due to the father's high-profile work with Coalition forces in Iraq and his opposition to militant groups there.

Deferrals and Extended Delays—the Human Impact

When a refugee's resettlement application to the United States is delayed due to security processing delays, or for other reasons,[99] USCIS sends a letter to the applicant that states that the case has been "deferred." The USCIS letter is written only in English, and provides minimal information about the reason for the deferral. (See Appendix I for sample copies of these deferral letters.) The "deferral" letter does not include any information on the timeframe for a decision.

While some refugees depart within a matter of days or weeks after receiving deferral letters, many do not.[100] The fact that some refugees leave relatively quickly after receipt of deferral letters leads some other refugees to assume that they too will soon depart. Yet this is not the case for all refugee applicants. In fact, Human Rights First interviewed refugees in Jordan who had been waiting up to two years after receiving deferral letters. Of course, there are various factors that can contribute to refugees' confusion, including the fact that many refugees are no doubt urgently looking forward to resettlement as a solution to their family's displacement and some may inadvertently misinterpret the limited written or verbal information that is provided to them. But given the lack of clarity in the deferral letters and the lack of information provided by the U.S. State Department's OPEs, refugees who receive these deferral letters are often left confused and some interpret the letters as acceptances. For example:

■ **Iraqi refugee family in living in the outskirts of Amman believed they would be resettled to Sacramento, and interpreted their deferral letter as resettlement approval**. They had fled in 2006 from Baghdad following threats they had received as a result of their mixed Sunni-Shi'a marriage.

Upon their arrival in Jordan, they registered with UNHCR and were soon after referred to the United States for resettlement. Human Rights First researchers interviewed the family in Jordan in April 2010. The family explained that they had been told by IOM in August 2009—eight months earlier—that their application for resettlement to the United States had been approved, and that they would be resettled in Sacramento. Human Rights First reviewed a letter that they had received from USCIS. While the letter was in fact a "deferral" letter, the family had interpreted this letter as an acceptance to the U.S. resettlement program. Based on this letter and their communication with staff at IOM, the family believed that they would eventually depart. The father, Hassan, told Human Rights First:

"IOM [now] says we are on hold because of [our] security check. IOM told us we should call IOM in Egypt for information. Every time I call IOM I spend money, and our future remains uncertain. They should tell Iraqis when we can expect to leave, so we know when we can sell our belongings. We don't understand; some people applied at the same time we did and they have already left."[101]

Such delays in resolving resettlement applications, and a lack of effective and transparent communication with the applicants regarding the timeframe for decision-making, undermine the ability of the refugees to plan their lives and care for their families. Some refugees—like Yusuf, the Mandean refugee whose case is profiled above—prematurely withdraw their children from school and sell their belongings in preparation for resettlement, only to have their potential departure deferred. When speaking about security clearance delays, a UNHCR representative in Lebanon stated that the delays can be extensive, and that for vulnerable cases "we are wasting people's lives."[102] Another example:

■ **Refugee family in Jordan sells furniture and prepares to leave for the United States following receipt of a deferral letter, but delays result in additional processing.** In Jordan, Human Rights First interviewed an Iraqi refugee—Anwar—who had received a deferral letter in 2008 and interpreted the letter as a notice of approval.[103] Anwar, along with his wife and other family members, had fled Iraq to Jordan after being threatened because of the couple's mixed marriage; the husband is Sunni and the wife is Sh'ia. The wife felt particularly threatened as they had been living in a Sunni area of Baghdad. In 2008, UNHCR had referred the family for potential resettlement to the United States and the family was interviewed by the U.S. OPE and by USCIS.[104] Two years later, Human Rights First researchers found the family still waiting in Jordan as the security clearance of the primary applicant—the father—was still pending. The father, Anwar, told Human Rights First: "After the last interview, IOM told us we could leave at any time, so I started to pack our bags and get ready. We sold our furniture because I was ready to leave—that was what IOM told me."[105] Since 2008 the family has had to undergo three medical exams as the exams kept expiring due to the extended delays. Human Rights First researchers specifically asked Anwar why he thought the deferral notice was an approval, and he responded, "We thought the deferral notice is an approval because sometimes people leave after two weeks...And I swear to god that when I was given the paper [by IOM] they said I should be ready to leave within two weeks."[106]

Interviews with Iraqi refugees after their resettlement to the United States also confirm that the deferral letters, and lack of information provided to refugees on processing delays, create significant difficulties for refugees who are slated for resettlement to the United States. For example, Hana, an Iraqi refugee who had been resettled from Cairo to the United States, told Human Rights First that she was aware of "many Iraqis who made

arrangements to leave Cairo before their security check was complete."[107] She reported that some sold their apartments and belongings and withdrew their children from school. Hana urged that "IOM should put more emphasis on the importance to not make any life alterations while awaiting the security clearance.[108] Another Iraqi refugee currently in the United States, Akbar, told a Human Rights First researcher that there was very little notice regarding his departure, which took place after a year of waiting for his security clearance. Akbar said, "You have to prepare yourself, everything, in one week."[109]

The delays in security clearances can also lead to the separation of families. One Iraqi refugee told a Human Rights First researcher that her family was separated due to the different waiting periods for individual family members—and the delayed approval of one family member as a result of the extended waiting time for security clearances. Part of the family—the mother and daughter—were accepted for resettlement to the United States and had their security checks cleared before the husband. The family decided that the mother and daughter should depart before they heard about the outcome of the father's security clearance. Luckily the father followed to the United States three months later after his security check cleared.[110] In additional interviews, Human Rights First was informed that there were other cases of refugee families who were separated due to these delays, and that in certain instances, after a family was split up the remaining family member was eventually denied resettlement.[111] The delays in security clearances can put families in untenable situations—forcing them to make difficult choices about whether some family members should proceed with their resettlement without yet knowing whether the complete family has been approved.

Unnecessary Delays Can Lead to Inefficiencies

In addition to causing serious difficulties for refugees and their families, delays in U.S. processing can also cause other inefficiencies in the USRAP. For example, delays can make it necessary for refugees to undergo repeated medical examinations as medical checks expire after one year. Moreover, while some security checks are being processed, other security checks can expire. Thus the long wait times for some checks can lead to a situation where other checks have to be repeated—an additional expense incurred by the U.S. government that could be avoided if all the processing could be conducted in a timely manner. Duplicative medical exams and repeated checks also require additional staff time. These and other inefficiencies could be reduced if all parts of the resettlement processing—including the security clearance processing—were conducted in a more timely and coordinated manner.

Unclear Guidance on Delays Provided by U.S. Government to Refugee Resettlement Applicants

As illustrated by the refugee experiences detailed above, the information on deferrals and delays provided by the U.S. government's processing entities (OPEs) can be inconsistent and in certain instances inaccurate. For example, Anwar, the Iraqi refugee interviewed by Human Rights First and quoted above, reported that he was told by IOM that he and his family should be ready to depart to the United States within two weeks but was still waiting for departure two years later. IOM and other OPEs themselves are also frustrated as they cannot provide additional or updated information on wait times if refugee applications have been deferred because they are awaiting security clearances. In this regard, one OPE representative told Human Rights First, "The lack of transparency undermines the credibility of the entire process. It is only in the interest of the U.S. resettlement program to provide more information."[112]

In interviews with the Department of the State in Washington, Human Rights First was informed that it maintains standard operating procedures (SOPs) which explain how refugees should be advised about delays and deferrals by OPE representatives. Human Rights First has requested to review these SOPs, but at the time of publication of this report, the Department of State has not provided a copy of any procedures describing how refugees should be advised of deferrals or delays. In addition, IOM—which operates under contract with the Department of State—advised Human Rights First that it is not aware of any guidance provided from any source on deferrals or delays.[113]

Current Security Clearance Process

The security clearance process is an inter-agency process that requires the participation of the Departments of Homeland Security, State, and Justice. Intelligence agencies including the Central Intelligence Agency are also involved in varying degrees depending on the applicant being screened. On May 29, 2007, DHS announced "enhanced security screening procedures" for Iraqi refugee applicants, beyond those screening procedures ordinarily conducted for all refugee groups.[114]

Current security clearance procedures often call for the conduct of a specific security check called a Security Advisory Opinion (SAO), which involves extensive analysis of names and birthdates within intelligence and other government databases.[115] Over the last seven months, Human Rights First interviews in Washington and elsewhere have confirmed that the SAO processing stage is where the most lengthy delays occur.

While some additional resources have reportedly been provided to help address the slow SAO processing times,[116] these delays have not yet been adequately addressed. In fact, Human Rights First was advised in August 2010 that the average SAO processing time for an individual Iraqi refugee is five months.[117] This amount of time is well over the 45 days which was stated by David Martin in 2005 as the time alloted for the completion of an individual SAO.[118] While Iraqi applicants may have their SAOs completed in less than the average processing time of five months, Human Rights First met a number of refugee families in Jordan, Lebanon and Egypt who had been waiting upwards of ten months just to receive their security clearance. The SAO process for Iraqi refugee cases can require additional staff time and attention because some Iraqis have common and/or multiple names, all of which must be individually analyzed and cleared. The process may also be extended for applicants whose security check processing results in a potential hit or match with a name in a government intelligence database. For these applicants, additional screening by different departments within multiple intelligence agencies may be required. A 2005 study commissioned by the Department of State explained that a positive "hit" in the State Department's Consular Lookout and Support System (CLASS) does not "necessarily mean that a person is inadmissible" as the negative information discovered may not actually relate to the person applying for resettlement.[119]

U.S. Government Bodies and Other Stakeholders Raise Concern About Extended Delays in the Security Clearance Process for Iraqi Refugees

Two U.S. governmental publications, both issued in 2009, confirm that delays in the security checks delay the resettlement processing of Iraqi refugees. In an April 2009 report on Iraqi refugees, the U.S. Government Accountability Office (GAO) reported that, according to the State Department:

- "if serious delays occur in any one [refugee] case, they are generally due to the time it takes to complete security clearances";[120]

- "about 53 percent of the Iraqi refugees who were approved for resettlement but have not left for the United States have not done so because State is awaiting completion of security clearances, known as security advisory opinions, from the Central Intelligence Agency"; and that

- insufficient personnel to process SAOs at the CIA had become a significant issue for many immigrant and refugee applicants, including Iraqis.[121]

In a set of recommendations issued in April 2009 on the adjudication of refugee resettlement applications, the Ombudsman for DHS's U.S. Citizenship and Immigration Services also noted that "some [Iraqi refugees] face extended processing delays due to security screening by other U.S. government agencies.[122]

In an April 2009 report entitled *Promises to the Persecuted,* Human Rights First highlighted the delays in security clearance processing for U.S.-affiliated Iraqis.[123] In a May 2010 report on the situation of U.S.-affiliated Iraqis, the List Project to Resettle Iraqi Allies reported that "a significant portion of bottlenecks and delays happen at the security processing stage."[124] The List Project report stated that these delays "make little sense for Iraqis who have already held sensitive positions, faced extensive background checks, and undergone polygraph examinations."[125]

More recently, State Department officials informed Human Rights First that they too are frustrated by delays in the SAO process—one called it "SAO hell."[126]

According to this official and other stakeholders, the Department of State is not always able to identify and/or address the cause of delays in processing. Given that the Department of State is the agency responsible for the overall coordination of U.S. refugee resettlement—and that it does hear about cases needing urgent processing—its inability to identify and address these delays in certain individual cases undermines its capacity to protect refugees facing imminent risk.

Conclusion

The delays that plague the multi-agency security process are leaving many Iraqi refugees in destitution, in dangerous or difficult circumstances and without information sufficient for them to understand when or if they will depart. The National Security Council should lead a comprehensive review of the security clearance process in order to identify the factors that lead to delays and the impact of delays on refugee protection. The review should involve agencies conducting SAOs and other clearance checks in Washington as well as the U.S. OPEs who are informing refugees of delays in countries of first asylum. The President should then commit the resources necessary to overcome the delays and ensure that the majority of security clearance checks for refugee applicants can be completed within a set timeline.

III. Iraqis at Risk on Account of their Affiliation with the United State

"The United States has a moral obligation to help those Iraqis who have assisted or are assisting our military and civilian forces."[127]

—Senator Carl Levin (D-MI), Chairman of Senate Armed Services Committee

From the early days of the war in Iraq, U.S.-affiliated Iraqis found themselves targeted with threats, harassment, kidnapping, violence and murder. Those Iraqis who chose to work for the U.S. government, military, or contractors, or for U.S.-based media groups or NGOs—who were crucially important to provide local expertise and language skills to the Americans—were quickly labeled as traitors by different militia groups inside Iraq. These employees were translators, journalists, researchers, fixers, drivers, members of the provisional reconstruction teams and staff at the U.S. Embassy, and their targeting became an instrument of battle. In 2008, the Congressional Budget Office estimated that there were 142,000 Iraqis who had worked as U.S. government contract employees or on USAID-funded programs.[128] An additional 4,000 Iraqis have worked for the U.S. Embassy in Baghdad or for U.S.-based media or NGOs.[129]

The threats these Iraqis face—from insurgent groups, militias, and terrorist organizations—have been well documented in the media. An in-depth examination by George Packer in the March 2007 *New Yorker* reported that kidnappings and murder of Iraqi interpreters were commonplace by 2004. In 2007, Ryan Crocker, then the U.S. ambassador to Iraq, reported that Embassy staff were facing direct threats as a result of their work with the United States, and argued that they should receive visas that would allow them to escape to safety.[130] While U.S.-affiliated Iraqis are not targeted today at the levels reported in 2006 and 2007, they remain at significant

risk in Iraq, along with many other Iraqis, including various minority groups.[131] Indeed, in July 2010, an Iraqi who reportedly worked for the U.S. military was murdered by his own son, a member of the Sunni insurgency who considered his father a traitor.[132] Other U.S.-affiliated Iraqis continue to be targeted for threats and violence. For example:

Driver for U.S. contractor was threatened with beheading and labeled a traitor. Mohammed worked for 16 months as a driver for a U.S. government contractor. He had fled Iraq, but ran out of money to support himself so had no choice but to return home in early 2010. For several months, he lived in relative peace and safety in Mosul, but then word got out that he was back in town. In June 2010, three or four carloads of men arrived at the door of his aging and infirm mother's house and demanded to see her son. They called themselves the "Muslim People of Islam," and have continued to visit her weekly ever since, telling Mohammed's mother that he is a U.S. collaborator and that they are going to cut off his head for treason. He has also received several direct threats over the phone from individuals who call him a traitor for working with the Americans. Mohammed's brother and sisters and some of his friends have asked him to stay away from them, to ensure the safety of their children. He is on the run, with his wife and children, staying only a night or two in any location.[133]

In November 2010, three years after he raised the clarion call to action on behalf of Iraqis at risk due to their U.S. ties, Ambassador Crocker spoke with Human Rights First and asserted, "I continue to believe we owe them special consideration."[134]

Two programs mandated by Congress in the Refugee Crisis in Iraq Act to create escape routes for U.S.-affiliated Iraqis have been operational since 2008. Almost three years later, our research indicates that these programs remain slow and inefficient. In an April 2009 report, entitled *Promises to the Persecuted*, Human Rights First evaluated implementation of both programs—the Special Immigrant Visa (SIV) program and the P2 program providing direct access to the U.S. refugee resettlement program. In that report, Human Rights First concluded that significant obstacles were undermining the effectiveness of the programs, which were assisting just a small percentage of the tens of thousands—or more—of U.S.-affiliated Iraqis in need.[135] Today, several thousand more Iraqis have arrived to the United States through these programs, and some bottlenecks in processing have been addressed. Despite this progress, however, many of the same problems persist, including:

- Excessively long processing times for both programs;

- Low application levels for the SIV program, indicating that the program remains underutilized; and

- Lengthy delays due to extended time required for security clearance processes.

The United States has a moral obligation to ensure that the SIV and P2 programs work as efficiently and effectively as possible. The late Senator Edward Kennedy (D-MA), who introduced the Refugee Crisis in Iraq Act with former Senator Gordon Smith (R-OR), said, "Regardless of where we stand on the war with Iraq, we are united in our belief that America has a fundamental obligation to assist the Iraqis who have courageously supported our forces and our effort in Iraq and whose lives are in peril as a result. The target of the assassin's bullet is now on their back, and our government has a responsibility to try to save their lives.""[136] Senator Smith spoke of "a national moral commitment to resolving the Iraqi refugee issue as quickly as possible."[137] Senator Carl Levin (D-MI), Chairman of Senate Armed Services Committee, stated,

"The humanitarian crisis caused by the millions of Iraqis who have been displaced is staggering... The United States has a moral obligation to help those Iraqis who have assisted or are assisting our military and civilian forces."[138] President Bush affirmed this obligation when he signed the Refugee Crisis in Iraq Act into law in February 2008. One year later, the newly elected President Obama recognized refugee and internally displaced families as "living consequence[s] of this war" and declared that "America has a strategic interest—and a moral responsibility—to act."[139] In fact, as instability and violence persist in the wake of the U.S. withdrawal, it is as important as ever for the United States to ensure that effective programs are in place to protect Iraqis at risk, including those who risked their lives to work with the United States or U.S. organizations.

Priority (P2) Access to the U.S. Refugee Program

The P2 program created by the Refugee Crisis in Iraq Act allows certain Iraqis to apply directly to the U.S. refugee resettlement program, without a referral from UNHCR. P2-eligible Iraqis include those who work or worked for the U.S. government, U.S. contractors or U.S.-based media or non-governmental organizations, and their close relatives, as well as persecuted religious or minority Iraqis with close relatives in the United States.[140] The P2 program does not reduce the legal requirements or security checks required for resettlement to the United States. All P2 refugee applicants are interviewed by USCIS officers to determine eligibility for resettlement, including whether they meet the refugee definition, present no known security risk, and are otherwise admissible to the United States under U.S. immigration law. They are able to apply for P2 resettlement from inside Iraq through a rare process known as "in-country" processing,[141] and can also apply from Jordan and Egypt. P2 processing is not available in Syria, where the vast majority of Iraqi refugees live, nor in Turkey or Lebanon, also home to large numbers of displaced Iraqis.[142]

P2 Resettlement Numbers

As of September 2010, a total of 7,649 U.S.-affiliated Iraqis had arrived in the United States through the P2 resettlement program, most directly from Iraq[143]—a significant (and overdue) increase since April 2009. At that time, only 1,398 U.S.-affiliated Iraqis had been resettled through the P2 program, as detailed in Human Rights First's 2009 report.[144] Despite this welcome increase, many more U.S.-affiliated Iraqis are still waiting for resettlement through this program. In fact, as of September 2010, more than 26,000 Iraqis are "in various stages of processing" of their P2 refugee applications, according to the State Department.[145] This backlog is clearly substantial.

Resettlement Processing Times

Total processing times for P2 resettlement applicants do not appear to have improved significantly over the past 21 months. The State Department declined to provide information on these processing times in response to a request from Human Rights First in July 2010.[146] However, *pro bono* attorneys interviewed by Human Rights First report that the P2 resettlement process for U.S.-affiliated Iraqis requires 12 to 21 months of processing time, with the longest amounts of time reported for applicants inside Iraq. In 2009, these attorneys had reported that the process took one to two years. These lengthy processing times are unacceptable given the program's goal to bring at-risk U.S.-affiliated Iraqis to safety. Indeed, in 2007, Senator Kennedy suggested before Congress that "eight to ten months" was too long to wait for "courageous Iraqis... who have worked with the American military, the staff of our Embassy, or with American organizations to support our mission in Iraq."[147] The bi-partisan sponsors of the Refugee Crisis in Iraq Act proposed the P2 and SIV programs—which were approved unanimously in the Senate—to reduce the wait for Iraqi refugees with U.S. ties. Current processing times do not live up to Congressional intent, and fail the very Iraqis that these programs were meant to support.

Special Immigrant Visa (SIV) Program

The Special Immigrant Visa (SIV) program for U.S.-affiliated Iraqis was modeled on a much smaller-scale SIV program for Iraqi and Afghan translators established in 2006.[148] SIVs provide another distinct route to enter the United States for Iraqis who have worked with the United States in Iraq. Unlike the P2 program, which is limited to Iraqis in Iraq, Jordan and Egypt, SIVs are potentially available to Iraqis in Syria and elsewhere. (The SIV program is an immigrant visa program, not part of the U.S. refugee program, though both programs share some eligibility requirements in the case of U.S.-affiliated Iraqis.)

The newer program—known as the Section 1244 SIV program—made available 5,000 SIVs per year for five years to Iraqis who worked for a year or more for the U.S. government or military, either directly or with a private contractor.[149] To be eligible for this program, Iraqis must also demonstrate that they are experiencing or have experienced an "ongoing serious threat" as a result of their work for the United States.[150] An SIV holder may move to the United States and will receive a green card (lawful permanent residence) shortly thereafter, which means that he or she is fully authorized to work. His or her spouse and children may also move to the United States.[151] The older 2006 SIV program, providing 50 SIVs per year for Iraqi and Afghan translators who worked for the U.S. government, remains operational as well.[152]

Special Immigrant Visa Numbers

Since the inception of the program and as of September 2010, the State Department has issued 2,524 special immigrant visas under the Section 1244 SIV program to Iraqis who worked for the U.S. government, military, or contractors (plus an additional 2,523 SIVs to their spouses and children, who are included in the applications of the principal applicants).[153] This represents a significant increase; in March 2009 only 641 Iraqis had been issued SIVs.[154] Despite the increase, the total number of SIVs issued to U.S.-affiliated Iraqis—2,524—is still only a small percentage of the 15,000 SIVs available under the Section 1244 SIV program for the first three years of the five-year program. Given the backlog in the P2 program of 26,000 applicants—many of whom would also be eligible to apply for SIVs—it appears that the SIV program continues to be underutilized.

SIV Application Process and Processing Times

Total processing times for SIVs do not appear to have improved significantly since the inception of the SIV program. The State Department did not provide information on these processing times in response to requests from Human Rights First.[155] However, according to Human Rights First interviews with *pro bono* attorneys who represent U.S.-affiliated Iraqis, the SIV process can take 9 to 17 months from start to finish.[156] In 2009, these *pro bono* attorneys had reported to Human Rights First that the process generally took a year or more.[157] The processing time for the I-360 form (the actual SIV petition) has decreased to just one to three weeks, thanks to prioritization of these petitions by USCIS, but the other steps of the process remain overly lengthy.[158]

The SIV application process is complex, even by immigration application standards. A delay at any stage causes delay in the entire process. The process consists of a number of steps, which are undertaken in the following order:

1. *Chief of Mission (COM) approval*: The applicant must obtain approval from the Chief of Mission (COM) of the U.S. Embassy in Baghdad. To do so, the applicant submits a letter of recommendation from a U.S. citizen senior supervisor which states that he or she is experiencing or has experienced "ongoing serious threats" due to employment with the United States, a State Department form DS-57, and a copy of his or her Iraqi passport. The COM reviews and verifies the applicant's documentation and notifies the applicant of approval or denial.

2. *DHS-USCIS application*: The applicant prepares and submits USCIS form I-360 (the SIV petition) by regular mail to DHS's Nebraska Service Center with the recommendation letter, COM approval form and a copy of the Iraqi passport with certified English translation. USCIS adjudicates the petition and forwards approved petitions to the State Department's National Visa Center.

3. *National Visa Center (NVC) processing*: The NVC contacts the applicant by email and requests additional documentation, including a Family Book (a document held by local governments and unknown to many Iraqis), Iraqi military records, all evidence that the applicant worked for or on behalf of the U.S. government, a police certificate from the locality where the applicant resided (if the applicant lived outside Iraq for more than six months after age 16), two photographs and two additional forms if the applicant wants to receive benefits in the United States post arrival.

4. *Visa interview*: NVC schedules a visa interview at the local U.S. consulate for the applicant, and a State Department consular officer interviews the applicant and family. The applicant must present original copies of previously submitted documentation plus written evidence that he or she intends to resign his or her current job to move to the United States within three months.

5. *Security clearance*: Security clearance for all immigrants and refugees intending to come to the United States is a complex inter-agency process that requires the participation of the Departments of Homeland Security, State, and Justice. Depending on the applicant, intelligence agencies including the CIA are also involved. According to the State Department, it is initiated early in the SIV application process.

In 2010, the National Security Council, with the cooperation of the State Department, initiated a review of the entire multi-agency SIV process to identify ways to improve its efficiency and effectiveness. In connection with this process, a group of *pro bono* attorneys and other non-profit groups—including Human Rights First—have identified a number of inefficiencies and potential improvements to the system—including:[159]

1. *Slower processing of Chief of Mission (COM) approvals and onerous requirements for approval:* The length of time that it takes for applicants to receive COM approval from the U.S. Embassy in Baghdad has increased from six to eight weeks (as reported in April 2009)[160] to about six months to one year, according to *pro bono* attorneys who are representing U.S.-affiliated Iraqis. (The State Department maintains that COM approval has been taking three to four months.) The contractor that facilitates COM approvals on behalf of the State Department often requests documentation that was not required previously to demonstrate SIV eligibility, and is not necessary or is not the type of documentation an Iraqi employee would be expected to have. For example, Iraqis have been asked to provide copies of the contract between the U.S. government and a major U.S. contractor—a document they would have no reason to possess and can be difficult or impossible to obtain. Iraqis have also been asked to provide copies of the same documentation on multiple occasions. The *pro bono* attorneys and non-profit groups have recommended that the COM approval backlog be eliminated and that these overly onerous requests be stopped.

2. *Absence of a single office or focal point to help an applicant or his or her legal representative follow up on a case.* Because the SIV application process involves numerous U.S. government agencies plus at least one government contractor, it can be quite difficult for an applicant to raise concerns or ask questions about the processing of his or her case. The *pro bono* attorneys and non-profit groups have recommended that the U.S. government establish a focal point with the authority to follow up on SIV applications with the relevant agencies. This kind of role is played by the USCIS Ombudsman's Office, which, upon request, seeks to facilitate processing of SIV and P2 applications, but that Office's authority is limited to USCIS.

3. *Lack of a formal review process of denials of COM approvals or the actual visas.* When the Chief of Mission denies the COM approval, or the local consular official denies a visa, the applicant receives little to no information regarding the reasons for the denial, which makes it very difficult for an applicant or his or her legal representative to request a review, if they believe the denial was made in error. The *pro bono* attorneys and non-profit groups have recommended that formal review processes be established for denials at both stages, including a requirement that applicants receive more information regarding the reasons for the denial.

The State Department recently—in late November 2010—committed to making numerous changes to the SIV process that could improve its efficiency and ensure that applicants receive fairer consideration.[161] It is too early to determine the impact of these changes.

Delays in Security Clearance Process

As detailed in Section II of this report, delays continue to hamper the inter-agency security clearance procedure, which remains the longest step in the process for both SIV and P2 resettlement applicants. Security checks—which are initiated by the U.S. government early in the application process—generally take up to an additional six months after an application has otherwise been approved, according to *pro bono* attorneys representing U.S.-affiliated Iraqis.

Conclusion

The SIV and P2 programs were created to provide routes of escape for Iraqis who face danger in their country because they worked with the U.S. military, government, contractors or U.S.-based NGOs or media organizations. The programs have brought approximately 12,700 U.S.-affiliated Iraqis to safety in the United States since their inception.[162] However, the one- to two-year wait time undermines the ability of the programs to achieve their objectives, as the delays leave at-risk applicants exposed to further hardship and violence, especially inside Iraq, where high levels of violence persist. Human Rights First has set forth, at the beginning of this report, specific recommendations to address the inefficiencies and delays that are hampering the effectiveness of the P2 and SIV programs (including some recommendations identified by *pro bono* attorneys and other non-profit groups, as detailed above), including the long delays in security checks that affect P2 and SIV applicants as well as other Iraqi refugees.

IV. Protection and Resettlement for Refugees at Imminent Risk of Harm

"At the individual level...resettlement can still mean the difference between life and death."

—Guy Goodwin-Gil[163]

While all refugees in need of resettlement would benefit from more-timely processing, some refugees face risks of harm in the very countries to which they have fled—risks so grave that emergency or urgent resettlement is needed to ensure the protection of their physical security. For example, in a small number of cases, individual refugees have faced acute threats of harm from host governments or threats from non-state actors which the host government is unable or unwilling to control, imminent threats of deportation back to persecution, or life-threatening medical problems that require immediate treatment unavailable in the country where the refugee is currently located. While the number of refugees in need of expedited resettlement is likely minimal, as detailed below, the need for effective and transparent emergency resettlement is a global concern impacting refugees in many parts of the world. Through its interviews with Iraqi refugees, Human Rights First has documented some examples of the kinds of imminent risks that may merit emergency or urgent resettlement.

Emergency Resettlement as a Global Need

The need for emergency or urgent resettlement to protect refugees who face imminent risks of harm is a global need. As UNHCR recently explained in a May 2010 paper, "threats of *refoulement* and other acute risks faced by refugees increasingly oblige UNHCR to resort to emergency resettlement."[164] Yet the countries that operate refugee resettlement programs, including the United States, have limited capacity to conduct resettlement on an emergency or urgent basis.[165] Globally, only about 700 places per year are available for emergency resettle-

ment.[166] These places are all provided by resettlement countries *other than* the United States.[167] The number of emergency resettlement places is highly limited given the need, which goes well beyond 700 places. In fact, by the middle of each year, the 700 emergency resettlement places are generally filled.[168] The lack of sufficient emergency resettlement spaces is a serious protection gap, as refugees who face life-threatening scenarios are left stranded in dangerous or life-threatening situations.

Refugees Who Face Imminent Risks

Many countries to which refugees first flee—known as countries of first asylum—neighbor the country of persecution. As a result, a refugee may still be at risk from his or her persecutors even in another country. Given the harsh living conditions and the lack of rule of law in many refugee-hosting countries, some refugees may face imminent risks to their physical security which may warrant emergency or urgent resettlement. Some examples of individual refugees who might require such resettlement may include:

- A refugee who faces an immediate risk of forced return to persecution;

- A refugee whose persecutor, which may be a state or non-state actor, follows the refugee to his or her country of first asylum with the intention of inflicting harm. Refugees with this profile can include prominent human rights activists or journalists as well as refugees who are believed to have learned of classified and/or sensitive intelligence-related information;

- A refugee who experiences serious violence or threats of violence from non-state actors in a country of first asylum. These refugees could include a woman who is at imminent risk of an honor killing or a refugee who faces an imminent risk of harm due to perceived sexual orientation or gender identity;

■ A refugee child who is at imminent risk of trafficking; and

■ A refugee with a life-threatening and acute medical problem that requires immediate treatment unavailable in the country of first asylum.[169]

Over the course of its research into the resettlement of Iraqi refugees, Human Rights First learned of a number of examples of Iraqi refugees whose cases appear to illustrate the need for expedited processing. For example:

■ **Three-year-old girl with life threatening medical condition in need of emergency or urgent resettlement**. In Jordan, Human Rights First interviewed an Iraqi refugee family which included a three-year-old daughter who is suffering from severe kidney disease. The girl's parents administered medicine to her intravenously, but this was only a short-term solution. The child required medical treatment unavailable in Jordan to save her life. While the family had registered and been interviewed for resettlement with UNHCR, when Human Rights First researchers met them they had been waiting over six weeks for a resettlement referral. A UNHCR representative informed Human Rights First that UNHCR was aware of the case and wanted to submit the family for resettlement; however, at the time there was a shortage of resettlement places for urgent medical cases. More broadly, Human Rights First was informed by UNHCR that they do not generally refer these types of cases to the United States due to the unpredictability of the processing time for U.S. resettlement applications;[170]

■ **Refugee women facing imminent risk of attack**. Through its interviews, Human Rights First was informed of a small number of Iraqi cases submitted to Canada's Urgent Protection Program from Syria.[171] The cases involved Iraqi refugee women who had been placed in shelters to protect them from family violence yet still had male family members actively searching for them with the goal of inflicting harm.[172] Similar cases in Jordan exist as well.[173]

■ **Refugees who face imminent risks due to their sexual orientation**. Throughout the region, lesbian, gay, bisexual, transgender and intersex (LGBTI) refugees who have fled persecution in their home countries face varying levels of discrimination and abuses in the countries to which they have fled in search of protection.[174] In some cases, an LGBTI refugee may also face an imminent risk of physical harm in these countries. For example, a gay refugee from Sudan was left stranded for many months in Egypt where he lived at constant risk of being arrested and jailed because he was gay.[175] This refugee, named Hassan, was arrested and jailed for a year after being charged with "habitual debauchery," a charge used by Egyptian authorities to arrest LGBTI persons.[176] After his release in April 2009, Hassan was referred for resettlement to the U.S. resettlement program. In July 2009, Hassan was informed that his case was deferred pending his security clearance, which took ten months to complete before his departure to the United States.[177] During this time, the police continued to monitor Hassan and he faced threats of re-arrest, as well as significant difficulties in securing safe housing.[178] Human Rights First learned of a similar case of an Iraqi refugee who fled within the region and experienced direct threats—including a threat that he would be killed—on account of his sexual orientation.[179] Following a resettlement referral from UNHCR, it took the U.S. government four months to process this resettlement application, and the applicant is now safely in the United States. While the U.S. government did work to expedite this case,[180] the resettlement still took four months—leaving the refugee at grave risk of harm due to the threats he had experienced.[181]

UNHCR's Evacuation Transfer Facilities

In 2007 UNHCR together with States began to explore different options for the temporary relocation of refugees who face emergency situations, including the establishment of Evacuation Transfer Facilities (ETFs). The ETFs enable UNHCR to evacuate refugees facing imminent harm to third countries, where the refugees remain temporarily while resettlement processing takes place.[182] ETFs now exist in Romania and the Philippines.[183] Burkina Faso and the Slovak Republic have also served as locations for individual transfers on an *ad hoc* basis, and UNHCR is holding discussions with both countries on formalizing these roles. UNHCR has also noted the need to open an ETF in the east Africa region.[184] UNHCR reported that as of January 2010, 492 refugees had been evacuated to the ETF in Romania, and 17 refugees have been evacuated to the ETF in the Philippines.[185]

The establishment of the ETFs is a welcome development in providing protection to refugees who require emergency or urgent resettlement. Yet these facilities have several inherent limitations, which are listed below. These limitations indicate that while ETFs serve an important purpose, they are not a substitute for strengthened emergency resettlement programs operated by states. Some limitations of the ETFs include:

- **Capacity:** The ETFs can only accommodate a very small number of refugees. The ETF in Romania has capacity for 200 refugees at any given time. The ETF in the Philippines has an even smaller capacity—it can hold 20 refugees;[186]

- **Medical cases**: While the ETFs maintain limited capacity to address health concerns, they are not hospitals. As a result, they are often not appropriate for refugees who have serious medical conditions that require immediate treatment;[187]

- **Evacuation processing**: Facilitating evacuation requests also takes time. In 2009, it took an average of 28 days for UNHCR to evacuate a refugee to the ETF in Romania.[188] This is due to "complex clearance formalities, coordination and logistic requirements and difficulties to secure travel documents."[189] Yet if an individual is facing a life-threatening emergency, he or she may not still be alive or may face serious danger if forced to wait a month;

- **Case selection and identification**: In order to ensure that refugees are actually resettled after being evacuated, UNHCR must seek the provisional approval from resettlement countries *before* an evacuation takes place. As a result, UNHCR has sometimes had to make "difficult choices" in regards to who is actually evacuated.[190] While a "few" refugee cases at the ETFs were rejected by resettlement countries, UNHCR thus far has been able to find alternative resettlement solutions for these individuals.[191] Of further concern is the lack of information provided to NGOs and UNHCR field offices on the types of cases which may warrant evacuation to an ETF.[192] Such information would enable NGOs and UNHCR's field offices to better understand under what circumstances an evacuation request would be appropriate;

- **Limited resettlement processing time**: Countries which host ETFs maintain rules on processing times. For example, at the ETF in Romania, processing must take place within six months from the time a refugee arrives to the time he or she departs to a resettlement country.[193] Some resettlement countries, including the United States, are unable to guarantee that processing can happen within this timeframe. While most cases have been processed within six months, processing for a number of cases has gone beyond the six-month limit.[194]

For all of these reasons, UNHCR has rightly questioned whether "the evacuation transit option is more appropriate for urgent cases rather than for emergency cases."[195] Moreover, as ETFs have also been used at the request of resettlement states to conduct processing in situations where they are unable to travel to a certain location to conduct resettlement interviews—due to security concerns or problems in obtaining travel visas—there is also a risk that the true function of the ETFs may become lost or confused.[196]

Evolving U.S. Policy and Practice on Emergency and Urgent Resettlement

The United States is currently reviewing its practices and the potential for developing a formal policy relating to emergency and urgent resettlement. In addition, in response to concerns about the lack of a formal and effective U.S. process for expediting the resettlement of at-risk refugees, the Department of State has initiated a working group to examine issues related to expedited resettlement.[197] This is a welcome step as the lack of a formal and transparent procedure on behalf of the United States to process resettlement cases on a emergency or urgent basis contributes to situations where refugees in emergency situations languish and wait for prolonged periods while UNHCR seeks to find a solution, of which there are few. As detailed below, several U.S. government studies, UNHCR, and a wide array of U.S.-based organizations with refugee protection expertise have recommended that the United States develop a more formalized emergency resettlement procedure.

The current informal approach to emergency resettlement by the United States is not described in any published or accessible U.S. government document. The Department of State has stated publicly that "on a case-by-case basis, individual applicants in need of expedited handling are processed on an accelerated schedule"[198]—yet this schedule is not available publicly. According to written information provided by the Department of State to Human Rights First and other non-governmental organizations, the current informal approach involves the Department of State working "at all stages of the process to achieve the timeliest resolution possible."[199] The State Department also informed Human Rights First and the same group of NGOs that the total estimated time for this type of processing ranges between two weeks to five

months,[200] and that the process includes a number of aspects. Expedited cases receive the first available appointment for pre-screening, USCIS interviews and medical checks.[201] Cultural Orientation requirements may be waived.[202] The precise resettlement processing timing will vary by processing location and depend on the operations of the OPE and whether the OPE has a presence in a particular country where the refugee is located.[203]

OPEs also maintain their own expedited procedures. For example, in Jordan, IOM reports that its staff utilize an "expedite" check box in WRAPS—the Worldwide Refugee Admissions Processing System—which advances expedited cases to the front of all processing queues.[204] IOM also maintains a list of cases in need of expedited processing that are "long pending" due to security checks, and submits this list weekly to the State Department. Certain cases are also tracked manually.[205]

The UNHCR Resettlement Handbook—which contains guidance from each resettlement country including the United States on its resettlement policies and procedures—does not provide clarity when it comes to emergency resettlement. It rather confuses the position of the United States on expedited resettlement. A Section titled "Emergency Cases" in the U.S. chapter of the UNHCR Resettlement Handbook states:

> "DHS and the Department of State have agreed to *specific procedures* for processing limited numbers of emergency cases each year. Emergency cases are defined as cases in which the risk to the refugee is so great that processing must be completed within seven days. All such cases must be referred by UNHCR offices in the field to the UNHCR Resettlement Office in Geneva, which refers the case to the designated USG authorities in Washington. Upon acceptance of the case, the USG will initiate processing on an emergency basis."[206] (Emphasis added)

A sub-section on urgent cases continues:

"The U.S. Program tries to be responsive to urgent cases. However, these cases must follow the same procedures outlined in Section 7 above [on regular submissions]. Processing may be expedited by the USG in appropriate situations."[207]

The information in the U.S. chapter of the UNHCR Resettlement Handbook does not appear to be accurate given the current U.S. approach as outlined above, and as a result the information is misleading. At the most basic level, while the U.S. government has an informal approach through which it may expedite a case, this kind of *ad hoc* approach is very different from a set of "specific procedures" which are referred to in the UNHCR handbook. The reference to a set of "specific procedures" may be a reference to a U.S. "protocol" on emergency resettlement that was introduced in 2000 but is no longer in effect.[208] In addition, the timeframe referenced in the UNHCR handbook—seven days of processing for emergency cases—is not consistent with current U.S. timeframes for expediting cases, which State Department officials have advised, as noted above, usually takes from two weeks to five months.

Concerns About the Current U.S. Approach on Emergency Resettlement

While the current informal U.S. approach to expediting cases can help some individual refugees, this approach is not a formal or transparent process. Moreover, the delays in the conduct of security clearances (discussed above in Section II of this report) also impact upon the ability of the United States to expedite resettlement cases on an emergency or urgent basis. In fact, USCIS—in response to its Ombudsman's recommendation that it publicly state the criteria by which USCIS expedites certain emergent cases, confirmed:

"In some situations, expediting a case is outside the control of the Department of State, UNHCR or USCIS...some required security checks are conducted by other agencies, and while the USRAP can request that these agencies expedite

the checks, the Department of State and USCIS cannot compel these agencies to complete their screening within a certain time frame.[209]

Thus, even if a refugee's resettlement is "expedited" by the United States, that refugee's security check may still be delayed for months, which will likely be too slow for individuals who face imminent life-threatening risks. In addition, while only limited information is available on the United States' informal approach to expediting resettlement cases, there appear to be a number of problems with the current approach, including:

■ **The United States cannot commit to complete processing of an emergency case within a specific time period.** As a result, UNHCR generally declines to refer the most urgent cases to the United States due to the lack of predictability in processing times;

■ **It is unclear how an emergency resettlement request can be initiated and what factors or criteria may make a case appropriate for expedited resettlement under the U.S. resettlement program.** As a result, non-governmental organizations, UNHCR offices and others who interact with refugees who may be in need of emergency or urgent resettlement have little information as to how to formally request an expedited process. In response to the USCIS Ombudsman's finding of "a lack of transparency surrounding how to request an expedited review of emergent cases and how those requests are evaluated,"[210] USCIS committed—in its July 2010 response to the recommendations—to provide information to the public on how to request expedited processing for a pending refugee case.[211] This information has not yet been provided, but will be a welcome step;

■ **The government does not consistently inform the applicant or his or her legal advocates when a case is being conducted on an emergency or urgent basis.** This lack of information causes immense frustration and confusion for refugees, and for their legal advocates who may continue to submit requests to the Department of State because they do not know that the case has already been expedited;

U.S. government studies, UNHCR and others affirm need for emergency resettlement program

■ **A Department of State-commissioned report**, conducted by David Martin, the current Principal Deputy General Counsel of the Department of Homeland Security, recommended that the Departments of State and Homeland Security "should work together to restore the capacity to act in a matter of days or weeks to approve and resettle refugee persons who are in grave and immediate danger and whose cases are referred by UNHCR or a U.S. Embassy. This procedure for urgent action cases should replace the use of parole to the greatest extent possible. Such cases will be exceptional and the volume of such cases can be expected to be quite low, thus making special arrangements feasible";[212]

■ The **USCIS Ombudsman of the Department of Homeland Security** found a lack of transparency in how to request an expedited process for resettlement in emergent cases and recommended that USCIS "publicly state, on the USCIS website and through stakeholder groups, the criteria by which USCIS expedites certain emergent refugee cases and how to access that expedited process";[213]

■ **UNHCR** recommended in a July 2010 paper that "resettlement countries establish or strengthen emergency resettlement progammes";[214]

■ **Fifteen civil society groups**, including refugee organizations such as Human Rights First, recommended in a March 2010 letter to the U.S. Secretary of State that a "formal and transparent fast-track process should be put in place to ensure the safety and protection...[of refugees] who face imminent harm or danger in their countries of first asylum."[215]

■ **Interview availability**. While the United States has acknowledged that OPEs may request an emergency USCIS interview to conduct a refugee adjudication—and the U.S. has in the past deployed officers to conduct emergency resettlement interviews—it remains unclear under what circumstances the USRAP would dispatch an officer to conduct an emergency interview or whether such an interview is a real possibility given that refugees in need of emergency resettlement may be staying in remote locations; and

■ **When emergency processing is unavailable, it is unclear how NGOs can make a request for evacuation to *Evacuation Transfer Facilities*.** In the absence of such information, ETFs are less effective at meeting the protection needs of refugees in imminent danger in countries of first asylum.

As the State Department and other agencies conduct their review of U.S. practice and policy on emergency resettlement, they should address the impediments noted above, with the most critical factor being time. Time is the critical tool in preserving the lives of those refugees who face acute threats to their physical security. As noted above, the Department of State has stated that its total estimated expedited processing time ranges from two weeks to five months.[216] Two weeks may assist a refugee who faces imminent danger, but five months is too slow for a refugee who faces grave or imminent risks to his or her life. In July 2010, the State Department informed civil society groups that "each [refugee resettlement] case is different and no guarantees can be made on how long a particular security check will take."[217] These comments indicate that—at least as of July 2010—the State Department still did not have the ability to provide a firm timeline on the security check stage of the resettlement process. In order to create an effective expedited resettlement process to assist refugees who face imminent danger, the U.S. government will need to establish a timeframe within which all stages of the process will be completed, including security checks.

Conclusion

The United States cannot continue to expect the limited emergency resettlement places provided by other countries or the Evacuation Transfer Facilities (ETFs) to meet the protection needs of refugees whose lives are in imminent danger. As detailed above, the need for expedited resettlement far exceeds the spaces that are made available by other States, and the ETFs (which are indeed very important initiatives) should not be viewed as substitutes for expedited resettlement systems. Moreover, there are important reasons for the United States itself to develop a formal and transparent expedited procedure of its own to resettle emergency cases. These reasons include:

- **A global model:** The United States is the leading resettlement country in the world and serves as a model for global resettlement policy and practice. Given this role, the United States should set a positive example through the establishment of an emergency program, especially as other countries look to the United States as they establish or refine their own programs;

- **Saving lives:** One of the most important functions of resettlement is to preserve the physical security of refugees. The United States has acknowledged this by stating that its "first priority" when it comes to resettlement is to ensure "the safety of refugees in urgent need of protection. Such refugees face serious threats to their physical security or have other urgent needs that cannot be met in countries of first asylum."[218] Without an emergency procedure which ensures expedited processing at every stage, the U.S. resettlement program lacks the infrastructure to ensure it is working towards its "first priority"; and

- **Protecting those with U.S. ties:** The United States has an interest in ensuring the protection, through resettlement when appropriate, of refugees who have strong U.S. ties—such as family, employment, community or other close U.S. ties—and are facing an imminent risk of harm. It would make little sense for example, for a refugee with two U.S. citizen siblings or a refugee who was being targeted due to his work with the U.S. government, to be resettled to Sweden simply because that country has an expedited resettlement program.

V. Access to Information and Transparency in the Resettlement System

"If I could just get a definite answer from them [UNHCR] regarding my case, I could plan my life, not just sit and worry and worry and wonder without being able to move forward or backwards."[219]

—Iraqi refugee who had been registered with UNHCR in Jordan three years ago and was still uncertain about the status of a possible referral for resettlement by UNHCR

In addition to the challenges outlined in prior sections of this report, some Iraqi refugees also face a number of challenges due to the lack of information provided- by both UNHCR and, for those referred for U.S. resettlement, the United States—about the status and timing of their cases, including applications and referrals for potential resettlement. Without regularly updated information on the status of their applications for resettlement, refugees are unable to assess their real options and are uncertain about how to best support themselves and their families. As detailed below, refugees are provided with inadequate information at several stages including:

- while they are waiting to be potentially referred for resettlement by UNHCR;

- after they have been referred by UNHCR for potential U.S. resettlement, but while their resettlement applications are still awaiting decisions by the United States; and

- when their applications for resettlement are denied by the United States.

This lack of information and transparency in decision-making cause significant frustration for refugees and can further the sense of despair and hopelessness that many of them may have about their futures. In addition, the lack of information can generate distrust among refugees of

the various agencies involved in resettlement processing. In its recommendations on the U.S. refugee resettlement program, the Department of Homeland Security's USCIS Ombudsman recognized many of these concerns and urged that USCIS undertake reforms to provide case-specific information to refugees if they are denied resettlement, as well as provide further guidance to denied applicants to enable the submission of meaningful reviews of initial decisions. The Ombudsman's recommendations are discussed further below.

Resettlement Referrals by UNHCR

Refugees from Iraq have fled to a number of different countries in the region that do not have domestic asylum systems. Syria, Jordan and Lebanon are not signatories to the 1951 Refugee Convention or its 1967 Protocol. As a result, UNHCR staff, rather than the host countries, conduct refugee status determinations in the region. While UNHCR currently recognizes Iraqi refugees who have fled from certain regions of Iraq on a *prima facie* basis,[220] this recognition does not translate into automatic eligibility for resettlement.

While UNHCR has referred over 100,000 Iraqi refugees for resettlement from the Middle East to resettlement countries since 2007,[221] there are many refugees who, for various reasons, are not referred for resettlement by UNHCR. For example, a refugee might not meet UNHCR's current resettlement eligibility requirements which aim to identify vulnerable cases in need of resettlement.[222] In addition, while a particular refugee may be considered a *prima facie* refugee given the governorate in Iraq from which he or she has fled, UNHCR will still not refer a case for resettlement if the refugee does not also have a well-founded fear of persecution within the meaning of the 1951 Refugee Convention. The United States and other resettlement countries will only resettle refugees who meet this definition.[223] UNHCR will also not submit a case for resettlement if its staff have concerns that the individual might have committed certain acts or crimes that would make him or her "excludable" from refugee protection.

When UNHCR does not refer a refugee for resettlement, its staff do not consistently inform that refugee that he or she has not been referred for resettlement. UNHCR has told Human Rights First that its staff do not provide this information because the resettlement criteria may change over time and as older case files are reviewed, some refugees who were not initially referred for resettlement may be referred at a later time.[224]

The practice of not informing refugees if they are not referred for resettlement generates confusion and frustration for refugees. For example:

■ **An Iraqi refugee who was only told his file is "under review" cannot plan for future.** An Iraqi refugee explained to Human Rights First researchers his frustration after waiting for three years in Jordan for a resettlement referral, and being told— in response to each of his multiple inquiries to UNHCR—only that his "file is under review."[225] This refugee, who had fled sectarian violence in Iraq in 2006, told Human Rights First in 2010, "If I could just get a definite answer from them [UNHCR] regarding my case, I could plan my life, not just sit and worry and worry and wonder without being able to move forward or backwards."[226]

■ **An Iraqi refugee interviewed by UNHCR six years ago was told only that his file is "on hold."** Human Rights First interviewed an Iraqi refugee who had fled Iraq to Jordan in 2004 along with his family due to religious persecution. This family are Sabeans. The Sabeans (also known as Mandeans) are a religious minority that has been targeted with brutal persecution in Iraq. After arriving in Jordan, he registered with UNHCR. The man told Human Rights First that he had been interviewed by UNHCR and issued an asylum-seeker certificate,

but when he asks UNHCR about the status of his case and chances for resettlement, he is continually told that his file is "on hold."[227]

UNHCR—Exclusion and Resettlement

An Iraqi refugee will also not be referred for resettlement if UNHCR learns, during its registration and refugee status determination processes, that there is reason to believe that the individual committed heinous acts or serious non-political crimes in the past. These acts—found in Article 1F of the 1951 Convention—exclude individuals from refugee protection if there are serious reasons for considering that they have committed:

■ A crime against peace, a war crime, or a crime against humanity, as defined in international instruments drawn up to make provision regarding such crimes;

■ A serious non-political crime outside the country of refuge prior to admission to that country as a refugee; or

■ Acts contrary to the purposes and principle of the United Nations.[228]

Those refugees who trigger strong exclusion concerns are issued asylum-seeker certificates by UNHCR and are also scheduled for individual refugee status determination interviews conducted by UNHCR's protection staff to enable UNHCR to determine if these individuals should be excluded from refugee protection.[229] Other cases that raise lesser potential exclusion-related concerns are issued refugee certificates and are only given refugee status interviews if there is a need for UNHCR to take some action with respect to the refugee, such as potentially referring the refugee for resettlement.[230] UNHCR's approach towards handling potentially excludable cases varies depending on location, and depends on the local protection context.[231]

Publicly available information on UNHCR's exclusion practice in the context of Iraqi refugees is highly limited.[232] In July 2010, Human Rights First requested that UNHCR make available the number of Iraqis excluded and the number of pending exclusion decisions, as well as provide information on the extent to which procedural fairness is part of how UNHCR conducts exclusion interviews and issues corresponding decisions. Elements of procedural fairness include informing the applicant that he or she is being considered for exclusion, an individualized determination including an oral hearing, access to legal assistance, disclosing relevant factual evidence and providing an opportunity to respond, providing the individual with a written decision including reasons for the decision and ensuring the right to an independent review process.[233]

While UNHCR has not yet—as of the time of publication of this report in December 2010—provided information requested by Human Rights First on these issues, the agency has publicly stated that the number of Iraqi refugees requiring exclusion interviews is "low," numbering between two to three percent of all Iraqis registered.[234] Two to three percent of the current number of registered Iraqi refugees ranges from 4,500 to over 6,000 individuals. This is not the number of refugees who have been determined to be excludable, but rather the number who require UNHCR interviews to determine if they should be excluded from refugee protection. UNHCR representatives have also informed Human Rights First that the number of Iraqis waiting for such interviews is greater than the number who have actually been determined to be excluded from refugee protection.[235]

Human Rights First did not interview any Iraqi refugee who had been formally excluded. While examining exclusion practices was not one of the objectives of Human Rights First's research in Jordan, Lebanon and Egypt, in conducting research on resettlement, Human Rights First researchers did interview Iraqis who, like those Iraqis quoted above, have been waiting for years to be referred for resettlement by UNHCR. Some of these individuals may have their case files pending by UNHCR due to concerns that they may potentially be excludable. Yet as UNHCR neither informs refugees if they will *not* be referred for resettlement nor informs them of why they are not being referred, these refugees did not have information

from UNHCR that would enable Human Rights First—or more importantly the refugees themselves—to discern with any certainty why their individual cases had not been referred for resettlement. The lack of information from UNHCR on its exclusion policies and procedures in the region makes it difficult to understand and analyze the impact of exclusion, as well as whether exclusion is being conducted in a manner that conforms to procedural standards of fairness.

UNHCR needs to take steps to strengthen the transparency of its decision-making as it relates to resettlement referrals and ensure its exclusion processes include procedural safeguards. A study published in November 2009 supported by CARE International in Jordan recommended that UNHCR inform Iraqi refugees if they are not going to be referred for resettlement as those who are not referred "would no longer wait interminably for an invitation by an embassy for an interview."[236] This study concluded that informing refugees that they will not be referred would enable these refugees to "more realistically consider their options for the future and cease hoping for an opportunity that does not exist."[237]

Resettlement Denials by the United States

Refugees who are referred by UNHCR for resettlement to the United States, but are found to be ineligible for resettlement after U.S. interviews, do not receive adequate information from the United States about the reasons for their denials. As a result, a refugee who may wish to submit a meaningful Request for Reconsideration (RFR) will often lack the very information necessary that would enable her or him to address the reasons for the initial denial. Human Rights First interviewed a number of Iraqi refugees in Jordan and Lebanon who did not understand the reasons that their cases had been denied.

When a refugee is denied resettlement after an interview by a USCIS officer, the refugee receives a "Notice of Ineligibility for Resettlement" form in English that contains a series of boxes for the adjudicator to check listing different possible reasons for denial. In October 2009, USCIS revised this Notice to include some additional boxes that allow USCIS officers to provide additional information as to the reasons for denial. For example, while previously a refugee was informed only that he or she was denied on the basis of credibility, now a refugee may also be told that his or her refugee claim was found not credible for a number of reasons, including because of his "refugee claim," or "qualification to access the USRAP."[238] Denied applicants may also now be told that they had insufficiently explained concerns about credibility during their interviews with USCIS in relation to, for example, "material inconsistencies" within their testimonies or inconsistencies between their testimony and other evidence, such as country conditions.[239] Yet these are still only very general explanations that do not provide the factual basis underlying USCIS's conclusions. Hence the level of information provided in these revised notices does not satisfy the recommendation of the USCIS Ombudsman's office that USCIS "articulate in the Notice of Ineligibility for Resettlement clear and case-specific information regarding the grounds for denial."[240] Indeed, the Ombudsman's Office found that "the new Notice's checkboxes for grounds do not necessarily help applicants understand the factual basis that caused the adverse determination."[241]

The revised Notice of Ineligibility is moreover still issued only in English. Refugees and OPEs, however, informed Human Rights First that the Notice is generally interpreted for the refugee into Arabic during a counseling session conducted by OPEs. Yet given that the Notice itself is only in English, Iraqi refugees cannot effectively review it after they leave that session, unless they are fluent in written English. Human Rights First also learned of one case involving an Iraqi applicant in Baghdad who was served with a Notice of Ineligibility via email from the OPE, and was only served with it in response to an inquiry that the applicant had made, and was not provided a translation of the content of the form.[242]

In the domestic asylum context, the current form of the Notice of Ineligibility follows the same general model (in terms of content and form) as the Referral Notices that the USCIS Asylum Office issues to applicants for asylum within the United States whose cases the Asylum Office is not granting and whom the Asylum Office is "referring" into immigration court removal proceedings. While the lack of clear information as to the basis for the adjudicator's conclusions is a problem in that context as well, and frustrating for many asylum applicants, the legal damage caused by this lack of information is limited by the fact that an asylum applicant in this situation is entitled to a new (or *de novo*) hearing on his or her application for asylum before the immigration court. In other words, vague though the Referral Notice may be, the asylum seeker is not put in the position of having to appeal, or request reconsideration of, this decision— rather, the immigration court will make its own assessment of the actual asylum claim. A better model for the Notice of Ineligibility for refugee resettlement would be the Notice of Intent to Deny that the Asylum Office issues to some asylum applicants (i.e. to those who are in valid immigration status at the time their claims are decided, and with respect to whom the Asylum Office's decision will be final at least for as long as the applicant remains in valid immigration status). These Notices of Intent to Deny provide the factual and legal basis for the decision, including an account of the adjudicator's understanding of the applicant's testimony, which allows the asylum applicant—linguistic and legal barriers aside—to know what the factual and legal issues are that he or she needs to address.

While the overwhelming majority of Iraqi refugees who are referred by UNHCR for potential U.S. resettlement are accepted for resettlement after their interviews with USCIS,[243] the examples below illustrate that for a refugee who is denied resettlement by the United States, the absence of specific reasons for the denial make it difficult to impossible for that refugee to submit a meaningful request for review or assess alternative options, such as possible resettlement to another country. This problem applies not only to Iraqi refugees, but to all refugees who are applying for resettlement to the United States. Moreover, given that refugees who are denied resettlement by the United States had already in most cases been recognized as refugees by UNHCR, the U.S.

denials are sometimes seen as arbitrary by applicants, particularly as the reasons for the U.S. denials are provided in only general terms.

U.S. Resettlement Denials on the Basis of Credibility

An Iraqi refugee woman—Samar—fled from Baghdad to Jordan in January 2008 along with her husband and daughter. After registering with UNHCR, the family was referred for resettlement to the United States. Samar's husband informed Human Rights First that the family had faced persecution in Iraq because he had worked on a U.S. military base. The family has been directly threatened by different militia groups due to the husband's work. In addition, Samar and her husband had been caught in a gun battle between the U.S. military and the Sadr militia which resulted in serious injury to Samar's face. During the battle, Samar was transported to a hospital on a U.S. military base in Iraq, and underwent six facial surgeries. Samar said that American military doctors had suggested that she and her family seek resettlement to the United States from Jordan. Following this advice, Samar and her family left for Jordan and she continued receiving medical care in Amman, with the help of Medicins Sans Frontières. When our researchers met her, Samar's face, which had already undergone multiple surgeries, was still heavily scarred. Her voice was also muted and strained by damage inflicted to her vocal cords. Following Samar's interview with USCIS she received a Notice of Ineligibility, indicating that her resettlement application and the application of her family was denied because of a "lack of credibility" (Samar was the primary applicant). The Notice provided no explanation of what information was not considered credible so she has no way of knowing what additional information or documentation might help to clarify the situation. She lives with the constant reminder of the trauma she experienced, and yet her story was not believed and she does not know or understand why.

As noted above, U.S. resettlement denials that are based on credibility are couched in general terms such as a lack of credibility due to the applicant's "refugee claim," or their "qualification to access the USRAP."[244] While USCIS does provide specific training to its officers on evaluating

credibility,[245] the explanations provided to refugees are still very general phrases that provide no real explanation. A refugee who receives such an explanation does not receive information that would allow him or her to address whatever concerns the adjudicator had about the individual's credibility. Without sufficient explanation, it is difficult for a refugee who has been mistakenly denied resettlement due to credibility issues to effectively request review as he or she does not know what miscommunication may need to be clarified or what additional information could be provided to address a possible misunderstanding. As she did not know the specific reasons behind her denial, Samar felt that she was not in a position to request a review of the resettlement denial decision.

According to USCIS, lack of credibility is the most common reason for denying resettlement to Iraqi refugees in the region.[246]

U.S. Resettlement Denials on the Basis of "Other Reasons"

Between 2004 and 2009, Yassin, who speaks excellent English, worked for a number of U.S. firms in Iraq. His work in Iraq made him a target of different insurgent groups and militias. Yassin and his family received many threats which caused his parents and sisters to flee to Syria in 2006. Yassin remained in Iraq and continued his work with U.S. groups until 2009. In May 2009 he finally fled Iraq to Jordan. In Jordan, he contacted IOM (the U.S. OPE in Jordan) about the direct access (P2) resettlement program for U.S.-affiliated Iraqis. Despite having copious photographs, certificates of service and other documentation corroborating his employment with different U.S. entities, in October 2009 Yassin learned that his application for resettlement was being denied by the United States "for other reasons." Additional information was not provided on the USCIS Notice of Ineligibility. Despite his many years of service to United States, Yassin did not file an RFR of this decision because—given the lack of information provided to him on the Notice of Ineligibility—the specific reasons for the resettlement denial were unknown to him and, as a result, he did not feel he could successfully refute these unknown reasons. "What would I put in my appeal, even if I were to file it?" he asked.[247]

U.S. Resettlement Denials on the Basis of the "Persecutor Bar" or Other Bars

Hisham, a young Iraqi man, arrived in Lebanon in 2006 following sectarian tensions and direct threats he experienced by different militia groups. After registering with UNHCR and being referred for resettlement to the United States, Hisham was interviewed by USCIS officers in early July 2008. Later that month, Hisham received a Notice of Ineligibility, indicating that his application for resettlement was denied due to the "persecutor bar." This notation refers to a provision of the U.S. Immigration and Nationality Act (INA) which bars from resettlement and other immigration benefits persons who ordered, incited, assisted, or otherwise participated in the persecution of others on account of race, religion, nationality, membership in a particular social group, or political opinion.[248]

Hisham did not understand what this notation meant. When Human Rights First researchers translated the term "persecutor" into Arabic for Hisham, he expressed shock and disbelief. After understanding the meaning of the term, he was confused and did not understand what the reasons were for this denial. While Hisham did serve in the military in Iraq, which was obligatory, there was no way for Hisham to know if his military service was the reason for his rejection.

Without knowing the reasons that USCIS believes the persecutor bar applies in a particular case, a refugee is denied a meaningful opportunity to clarify any misunderstandings or provide relevant information through a request for review.

Hisham's case is not an isolated incident. Human Rights First interviewed another Iraqi refugee in Jordan who also received a Notice of Ineligibility that stated without explanation that his resettlement request was denied based on the "persecutor bar." This refugee worked for the Iraqi Department of Education. He could only conjecture

that his Ba'ath party membership may have been the cause of the denial decision. He told Human Rights First researchers, "I had to be a Ba'ath party member to work in the government, and I used to inspect schools. I never interrogated anyone or reported on any person. How could they say I persecuted others?"[249] Like Hisham, this Iraqi refugee was not provided enough information to prepare and submit a meaningful request for review of his denial.

USCIS guidance on applying the persecutor bar is not publicly available.[250] According to USCIS, this information has not been made public due to a concern that if the guidance were public, then refugees would withhold or alter information provided to adjudicators.[251] While attempting to ensure that refugees do not withhold potentially incriminating evidence or alter information is certainly valid, this interest should also be balanced with the need for individual refugees to confront evidence which lead to resettlement denials if they are to have a meaningful right to request review of those denials.

The lack of factual information does not apply only to the persecutor bar. Human Rights First is aware of two cases in which Iraqi refugees who had no involvement in terrorist acts were issued Notices of Ineligibility stating only that they had been found to be inadmissible to the United States under section 212(a)(3)(B)(i)(I) of the INA, which makes an alien ineligible if he or she has "engaged in terrorist activity." The Notices provided no legal information as to the content of that provision of law or the facts of the applicants' cases that led USCIS to conclude that they were inadmissible under that heading.

The Request for Reconsideration (RFR) Process

Globally, the vast majority of refugees denied resettlement by the United States do not submit RFRs. Of the roughly 16,124 refugee applicants from around the world who were denied resettlement by the United States in fiscal year 2009, only a small minority—approximately 2500—submitted RFRs.[252]

Most of the Iraqi refugees Human Rights First interviewed who were denied resettlement did not submit RFRs. While some refugees who are denied resettlement may not wish to submit RFRs, the low rate of RFR submissions is not only due to the limited information provided to refugees upon denial, but also likely due to a range of RFR processing problems, including a lack of guidance provided to refugees on how and where to submit RFRs.[253] In this regard, the USCIS Ombudsman has recommended that USCIS provide formal guidance on how refugees can submit a RFR, including what supporting documentation to file, where to submit the requests and that receipt of RFR submissions should be acknowledged in writing.[254] USCIS has concurred with these recommendations and expects to produce a standardized "tip sheet" on RFRs that will be posted on the USCIS website and distributed by the fourth quarter of FY2010. In FY 2009, USCIS also piloted a new quality assurance program for refugee adjudications which will provide USCIS means to determine whether refugee applicants are being given appropriate notice of potentially adverse decisions during interviews.[255] These steps are welcome.

The RFR process is also made more difficult for refugees as legal representatives are not allowed to attend USCIS interviews. While the vast majority of refugees seeking resettlement have no access to legal representation, a very small number do—for example through *pro bono* efforts aimed at providing legal assistance to U.S.-affiliated Iraqis and through a small number of legal assistance groups. But even for the few refugees who do have legal counsel, since these legal representatives are not permitted to attend USCIS resettlement interviews, these representatives generally have to rely on the refugees themselves to recall details of the proceedings as well as identify any points of contention.[256] However, while denied refugees may able to speculate as to why their applications were deemed ineligible based on the interview and the questions posed by USCIS, these non-lawyers are likely to have little or no awareness from the interview of what the interviewer's technical legal concerns were with the case. Moreover, the stress of the interview itself and the traumatic nature of revisiting the details of the refugee's past persecution may also undermine his or her ability to recall much after the interview. These difficulties compromise the ability of the few legal representatives who are working with refugees on their resettlement applications to submit RFRs, as they have little information as to what transpired during the interview.[257]

Conclusion

The Department of Homeland Security's USCIS Ombudsman shares many of these concerns. In an April 2010 set of recommendations on the adjudication of applications for refugee status, the Ombudsman recommended that USCIS 'articulate in the Notice of Ineligibility for Resettlement clear and case-specific information regarding the grounds for denial."[258] In its formal response to this recommendation, USCIS partially concurred, stating that they are "committed to providing refugee applicants with clear information on the reasons they were found ineligible for resettlement."[259] Following the introduction of the revised Notice of Ineligibility in October 2009, USCIS stated it will assess whether to revise the Notice of Ineligibility again after considering feedback from stakeholders.[260]

Appendix I
Sample Deferral Notices

American Embassy, Athens, GR
PSC 108, Box 25
APO AE 09842

**U.S. Citizenship
and Immigration
Services**

Date:
A-file Number(s):

NOTICE OF DECISION DEFERRAL

Dear M

Please be advised that a final decision regarding your application for refugee status in the United States has been deferred pending one of the following actions that will allow a final decision in your case:

☐ Verification of the documents presented at your interview

☐ Clarification from UNHCR about information you provided during your interview.

☐ Verification of relationship from your relative's case file in the United States.

☒ Completion of security review(s).

☐ Other:_____

At this time it is not possible to estimate how long it will take to make a final decision on your case. U.S. Citizenship and Immigration Services will send you a letter notifying you of the final decision on your application.

Sincerely,

Georgia Papas
Officer in Charge

American Embassy, Athens, GR
PSC 108, Box 25
APO AE 09842

**U.S. Citizenship
and Immigration
Services**

Date:
A-file Number(s):

NOTICE OF DECISION DEFERRAL

Dear M

Please be advised that a final decision regarding your application for refugee status in the United States has been deferred pending one of the following actions that will allow a final decision in your case:

☐ Verification of the documents presented at your interview

☐ Clarification from UNHCR about information you provided during your interview.

☐ Verification of relationship from your relative's case file in the United States.

☒ Completion of security review(s).

☒ Other: _further processing_

At this time it is not possible to estimate how long it will take to make a final decision on your case. U.S. Citizenship and Immigration Services will send you a letter notifying you of the final decision on your application.

Sincerely.

Officer in Charge

Appendix II
Recommendations for Improving Resettlement of Refugees upon Arrival in the United States—the Need for Structural Reform

While Human Rights First's research focused on U.S overseas refugee resettlement processing, in interviewing Iraqi refugees who had already been resettled to the United States about their experiences with the resettlement system, Human Rights First also gained information about the challenges they faced *after* their arrival in the United States. The challenges faced by Iraqi refugees resettled to the United States—many of whom are highly educated and/or victims of severe war trauma—serve to highlight current areas of concern in the U.S. domestic resettlement system overall.

Refugee Council USA, a coalition of refugee rights and faith-based service organizations (of which Human Rights First is a member), is currently advancing a range of recommendations to improve the U.S. resettlement program (USRAP) so that it may better deliver services to newly arrived refugee individuals and families.[261] As the White House continues to conduct its "comprehensive review" of the USRAP,[262] Human Rights First urges that these and other recommendations highlighted below—many of which were informed by Human Rights First's interviews with resettled Iraqis—are duly considered. The recommendations below are particularly pertinent for the Iraqi refugee population but if implemented would greatly assist all refugees resettled in the United States.

Expanded "Cultural Orientation" to Ensure Refugees Receive a Realistic Overview of Life in the United States

The "Cultural Orientation" (CO) training that refugees receive before their departure to the United States should better address the reality of life in the United States, including an overview of the domestic resettlement process upon arrival and an accurate portrayal of employment opportunities available in the United States. Refugees without any English language skills would benefit enormously from English as a Second Language (ESL) training prior to departure.

The Department of State is currently in the process of "revising the three-day orientation programs in Syria, Jordan, and Egypt to better fit the needs of Iraqi refugees."[263] As the Department has acknowledged, CO should ensure that refugees are fully briefed on "realistic expectations of life in America."[264] CO should be extended in duration and supplemented to include English language instruction and, ideally, region-specific information as a refugee resettled to Brooklyn, New York, will inevitability have a different acculturation experience than one who is resettled to Bowling Green, Kentucky. Resettled Iraqi refugees interviewed by Human Rights First researchers for this report reported that the CO did not adequately prepare them for life in the United States, and some refugees reported having received no CO at all prior to departure.[265]

Based on Human Rights First interviews with Iraqis resettled within the past two years, a more comprehensive CO program cannot be fully implemented without improved coordination of processing, including the need to provide advance notification of travel dates to refugees. A refugee who is given notice of only a few weeks or even days prior to his or her departure is put at a major disadvantage when it comes to properly preparing for life post arrival. As to be expected, he or she may not be in a position to take advantage of CO when rushing to vacate property, pack and make preparations to leave the country of first asylum. Of course, time will be limited in resettlement cases that are expedited, but odds of successful integration will increase through providing as much advance notice as possible and as comprehensive a CO as possible.

Increased Funding for Federal Resettlement Assistance

Human Rights First, along with many others, has welcomed the recent doubling of the Reception & Placement (R&P) grant from $900 to $1800 per refugee effective January 1, 2010.[266] The R&P grant is administered by the Department of State and is "intended to address challenges refugees face in their first 30-90 days in the United States."[267] The R&P funds "ensure that, in the first weeks after their arrival, refugees have a solid roof over their heads, a clean bed in which to sleep, and basic assistance."[268] The increase in the R&P grant is a critical first step in providing improved vital services to refugees during the initial resettlement phase, but additional reforms are also needed. For example, resettlement agencies are stretched thin: case workers have seen their refugee caseloads increase without a corresponding increase in immediate employment opportunities for their new clients, and the increased R&P grant remains inadequate to address immediate post-arrival needs.[269] One refugee interviewed for this report expressed so much frustration over the lack of initial financial assistance and economic opportunity in the months following his arrival that he considered returning to Iraq.[270] Human Rights First is aware of other Iraqis who have returned to Iraq—despite fears for their safety—because of the difficulty in finding employment and supporting themselves in the United States.

Increased funding for employment services and case management—to be adjusted each year for inflation—is necessary to provide refugees the chance to fully adjust to life in the United States and maximize opportunities for self-sufficiency.[271] When the refugee resettlement program began the in 1980s, cash assistance was provided to refugees for 36 months. Over the decades the pace of funding has not kept up with the needs of refugee clients, nor inflation. It is recommended that cash assistance be provided to all refugees for at least 12 months, up from the current maximum of 8 months.[272]

Additionally, funding should be appropriated for the Office of Refugee Resettlement within the Department of Health and Human Services to provide case management to all refugees for one year, and extended case management to especially vulnerable refugee clients who may need additional assistance in their adjustment and integration process.[273]

Implementation of Pre- and Post-Arrival Precautionary Measures to Identify Cases with Particular Needs

Refugees with specific needs, such as those who have survived trauma or torture, single women, refugees with health problems, LGBTI refugees and others, require appropriate and sensitive services to support their full integration. Ensuring that such services are in place will especially benefit refugees whose resettlement to the United States has been expedited due to life-threatening protection needs. Refugees with health problems, for example, should be resettled to locations where they can connect to appropriate health and community-based services to improve their quality of life.

In addition to the general case history and biodata which is already provided to resettlement agencies, these agencies should also be notified in advance of cases requiring specialized or particular support so that they may plan case management and acculturation services appropriately. As has been previously stated, "the proper identification, transfer, and use of this information is essential for resettled refugees to be placed with resources that meet their needs and, by extension, help them to become sustainably self-sufficient and achieve long-term integration."[274] The appropriate geographic placement of special cases, should these refugees opt for placement in specific sites, should also lessen the instance of "secondary migration," or the relocation of a refugee case from one region in the United States during the initial federal assistance phase.[275]

Pathways to Professional Opportunities for Highly Skilled Refugees

Many refugees who come to the United States with advanced degrees and a lifetime of professional experience find themselves in a position where their skills and expertise are never utilized in the American workforce. Iraqi refugees, many of whom were established professionals or academics in Iraq, are in particular need of a pathway to professional recertification. Among them—former doctors, engineers, professors and other specialized professionals—have found themselves resettled into situations of prolonged entry-level employment which do not provide opportunities for advancement. Allocated funding at the federal and/or state level targeted to refugee professionals would ensure that they are able to maintain and utilize their professional skills while effectively contributing to the American workforce.[276]

While the U.S. government does currently offer a federally funded Matching Grant program for qualified newly arrived refugees to "attain economic self-sufficiency within four to six months from date of arrival into the United States," this program is for immediate, short-term employment only. Funded by the Office of Refugee Resettlement, Matching Grant requires that affiliates of resettlement agencies match federal funds in the form of goods and services to qualified refugees within the first few months of arrival.[277] Refugees in this program are required to accept entry-level employment as an alternative to public assistance.

Overstretched resettlement agencies do not have the capacity to advise professional refugees on ongoing recertification procedures, specialized job placement or other long-term employment objectives. Agencies that do specialize in professional immigrant certification, such as Upwardly Global or RefugeeWorks, are region-specific and are unable to provide their services on a national basis.[278]

Elimination or Partial Suspension of Refugee Travel Loans

Refugees resettled in the United States are offered interest-free travel loans from IOM which they must pay back within 46 months after arriving in the United States.[279] This additional financial burden should be eliminated or temporarily suspended during the current economic downturn.[280]

Endnotes

[1] On October 31, 2010, gunmen seized the Our Lady of Salvation Church in Baghdad during a Sunday mass, taking over a hundred hostages. When Iraqi security forces attempted to free the hostages, approximately 50 individuals were killed, including priests, infants and police. See "Iraq church raid ends with 52 dead," Reuters.com, November 1, 2010, available at http://www.reuters.com/article/idUSTRE69U1YE20101101 (accessed December 10, 2010).

[2] Jack Healy, New York Times, "Coordinated Bombings Strike Across Baghdad," New York Times, November 2, 2010, available at http://www.nytimes.com/2010/11/03/world/middleeast/03iraq.html?ref=iraq (accessed December 9, 2010).

[3] UNHCR, Statistical Report on UNHCR Registered Iraqis, October 31, 2010, available at http://www.iauiraq.org/documents/1148/Monthly%20Statistical%20Report%20on%20UNHCR%20Registered%20Iraqis%2031%20Oct%202010.pdf (accessed December 10, 2010).

[4] Ibid.

[5] UNHCR, "Iraqi refugees regret returning to Iraq, amid insecurity," October 19, 2010, available at http://www.reliefweb.int/rw/rwb.nsf/db900sid/MDCS-8A2DWJ?OpenDocument&rc=3&cc=irq.

[6] Ambassador Crocker raised these points in a classified cable—which was provided to the Washington Post in September 2007, see Spencer Hsu and Robin Wright, "Crocker Blasts Refugee Process," Washington Post, September 17, 2007, available at http://www.washingtonpost.com/wp-dyn/content/article/2007/09/16/AR2007091601698.html (accessed December 10, 2010).

[7] In its 2010 Annual Report, the U.S. Commission on International Religious Freedom found that "systematic, ongoing and egregious religious freedom violations continue in Iraq. Members of the country's smallest religious minorities still suffer from targeted violence, threats, and intimidation, against which they receive insufficient government protection," see U.S. Commission on International Religious Freedom, Annual Report, May 2010, available at http://www.uscirf.gov/images/ar2010/iraq2010.pdf (accessed December 10, 2010).

[8] Anthony Shadid, "Church Attack Seen as Strike at Iraq's Core," New York Times, November 1, 2010, available at http://www.nytimes.com/2010/11/02/world/middleeast/02iraq.html.

[9] James A. Baker III and Lee H. Hamilton, The Iraq Study Group Report (New York: First Vintage Books, 2006), p. 87. Available at http://cspan.org/pdf/iraq_study_group_report.pdf (accessed December 10, 2010).

[10] See remarks by Senator Gordon Smith (R-OR) before the U.S. Commission on International Religious Freedom hearing entitled "Sectarian Violence in Iraq and the Refugee Crisis," September 19, 2007, available at http://www.uscirf.gov/component/content/article/160-iraq-press-releases/2158-hearing-on-sectarian-violence-in-iraq-and-the-refugee-crisis-remarks-by-senator-gordon-smith-r-or.html (accessed December 14, 2010).

[11] Press release, "Levin Applauds Inclusion of Iraqi Refugee Legislation in Defense Bill Conference Report," December 7, 2007, available at http://levin.senate.gov/newsroom/release.cfm?id=288555 (accessed December 14, 2010).

[12] See "Remarks of President Barack Obama -Responsibly Ending the War in Iraq," Camp Lejeune, North Caroline, February 27, 2009. Available at: http://www.whitehouse.gov/the_press_office/Remarks-of-President-Barack-Obama-Responsibly-Ending-the-War-in-Iraq/ (accessed December 2, 2010)

[13] Bureau of Population, Refugees and Migration, U.S. Department of State, "Doing Right by Newly Arrived Refugees " news release, January 22, 2010, available at http://www.state.gov/g/prm/rls/news/136429.htm (accessed December 5, 2010).

[14] In its formal response to recommendations on refugee applications from the Ombudsman of the U.S. Citizenship and Immigration Services, USCIS committed to undertaking a series of reforms which are outlined in Section IV and V of this report. For the formal USCIS response, see "USCIS Memorandum, "Response to Recommendation 44, Emergent or Denied Refugee Applications: Expediting Cases, Articulating Reasons for Denial, and Issuing Guidance for Requests for Reconsideration," July 2010, available at http://www.uscis.gov/USCIS/Resources/Ombudsman%20Liaison/Responses%20to%20Formal%20Recommendations/cisomb-2010-response44.pdf (accessed December 2, 2010), p. 2.

[15] Email correspondence with State Department official, September 10 2010. On that date, there were 411 Iraqis in Egypt and 966 Iraqis in Jordan moving through the P2 process. In Iraq, the number was approximately 25,000.

[16] Human Rights First interviews with *pro bono* attorneys representing U.S.-affiliated Iraqis, July 2010.

[17] Human Rights First email correspondence with State Department official, August 3, 2010. Endnote 117 below further elaborates the content of the email correspondence.

[18] U.S. Government Accountability Office, "Iraqi Refugee Assistance: Improvements Needed in Measuring Progress, Assessing Needs, Tracking Funds, and Developing an International Strategic Plan," April 2009, available at http://www.gao.gov/new.items/d09120.pdf (accessed December 2, 2010) p. 33.

[19] This case is detailed in Section II, p. 22, of this report

[20] Ibid.

[21] These cases are detailed in Section II, p. 23, of this report.

[22] Human Rights First, *Promises to the Persecuted: The Iraqi Refugee Crisis in Iraq Act of 2008* (New York: Human Rights First, 2009), available at http://www.humanrightsfirst.org/wp-content/uploads/pdf/090428-RP-iraqi-progress.pdf (accessed December 5, 2010).

[23] Human Rights First telephone interviews with *pro bono* attorneys, July 2010.

[24] In April 2009, this stage took just six to eight weeks. See Saurabh Sanghvi, "Abandoned in Baghdad," *New York Times*, August 30, 2010, available at http://www.nytimes.com/2010/08/31/opinion/31sanghvi.html (accessed December 10, 2010) for further discussion of problems with COM approval process.

[25] Human Rights First telephone interviews with *pro bono* attorneys, July 2010

[26] See State Department Fact Sheet data as of September 30, 2010, available at http://www.travel.state.gov/pdf/SQNumbers0910.pdf (accessed December 2, 2010)

[27] Human Rights First, *"Promises to the Persecuted,"* p. 11.

[28] Edward M. Kennedy (D-MA). *Congressional Record*, p. S15613 (December 14, 2007).

[29] Press release, "Kennedy, Smith, Levin, Brownback on the Iraqi Refugee Provisions in the Defense Authorization Conference Report," December 7, 2007., available at http://www.allamericanpatriots.com/48738702_kennedy-smith-levin-brownback-iraqi-refugee-provisions-defense-authorization-conference-rep (accessed December 3, 2010).

[30] Emergency resettlement and emergency resettlement places are elaborated and discussed in detail on pages 35-37 of this report.

[31] UNHCR, "Information Note and Recommendations from UNHCR: Emergency Resettlement and the Use of Temporary , Evacuation Transit Facilities" May 19, 2010, available at http://www.unhcr.org/refworld/docid/4bf3adfb2.html (accessed December 13, 2010), p. 9.

[32] These cases are described in detail section IV, pg. 36 of this report.

[33] The U.S. Department of State has described its approach to expedited resettlement in a recent U.S. report to Congress; see Department of State, U.S. Department of Homeland Security, U.S. Department of Health and Human Services, *"Proposed Refugee Admissions for Fiscal Year 2011, Report to the Congress*, available at http://www.state.gov/documents/organization/148671.pdf (accessed December 2, 2010).

[34] USCIS Ombudsman, "Recommendation Regarding the Adjudication of Applications for Refugee Status," April 2010, available at http://www.dhs.gov/xlibrary/assets/cisomb_recommendation_43_adjudication_refugee_status.pdf (accessed December 10, 2010), p. 2.

[35] USCIS Memorandum, "Response to Recommendation 44, Emergent or Denied Refugee Applications: Expediting Cases, Articulating Reasons for Denial, and Issuing Guidance for Requests for Reconsideration," July 2010, available at http://www.uscis.gov/USCIS/Resources/Ombudsman%20Liaison/Responses%20to%20Formal%20Recommendations/cisomb-2010-response44.pdf, (accessed December 2, 2010), p. 2.

[36] "Estimated Time Frames For Expedited Cases," distributed by Department of State representatives to civil society groups on July 12, 2010.

[37] David Martin, *The United States Refugee Admissions Program: Reforms for a New Era of Refugee Resettlement* (Washington, D.C.: Migration Policy Institute, 2005) p. 55.

[38] USCIS Memorandum, "Response to Recommendation 44," p. 2.

[39] USCIS Ombudsman, "Recommendations Regarding... Refugee Status," p. 2.

[40] This case is detailed in Section V, p. 47 of this report. In addition, and as detailed in Section V of this report, USCIS has issued a revised notice of ineligablity for resetttlement, which provides additional information to denied applicants, but this additional information is still only provided in general terms.

[41] This case is detailed in Section V, p. 47-48 of th s report.

[42] Ibid.

[43] JSCIS Memorandum, "Response to Recommendation 44," p. 5.

[44] UNHCR, "Iraq Fact Sheet," October 2010, available at http://www.iauiraq.org/documents/1151/Return%20Update%20IRAQ%20OCT%202010.pdf, (accessed December 2, 2010), p. 2.

[45] UNHCR, "Statistical Report on UNHCR Registered Iraqis," October 2010, available at attp://www.iauiraq.org/documents/1148/Monthly%20Statistical%20Report%20on%20UNHCR%20Registered%20Iraqis%2031%20Oct%202010.pd f (accessed December 13, 2010).

[46] Ibid.

[47] UNHCR, "Statistical Report on UNHCR Registered Iraqis."

[48] UNHCR, "Iraq Operation Monthly Statistical Update on Return,' June 2010, p. 1.

[49] U N., "Regional Response Plan for Iraqi Refugees" January 2010, available at http://www.reliefweb.int/rw/RWFiles2010.nsf/FilesByRWDocUnidFilename/AMMF-7ZNV7B-full_report.pdf/$File/full_report.pdf , p 9 (accessed December 1, 2010).

[50] UNHCR, "Iraqi refugees regret returning to Iraq, am d insecurity," October 19, 2010, available at http://www.reliefweb.int/rw/rwb.nsf/db900sid/MDCS-8A2DWJ?OpenDocument&rc=3&cc=irq (accessed December 2, 2010).

[51] Ibid.

[52] Human Rights First interview with Iraqi refugee, Amman, Jordan, April 21, 2010.

[53] Human Rights First interview with Iraqi refugee, Amman, Jordan, April 16, 2010.

[54] Although Lebanon's 1962 Law Regulating the Entry and Stay of Foreigners in Lebanon and their Exit from the Country provides that foreigners "whose life or freedom is in danger for political reasons" may request political asylum in Lebanon, these provisions in Lebanese domestic law have never been implemented either by the establishment of regulations or a governmental infrastructure for examining refugee claims and granting asylum, see articles 26-31, *Loi du 10 juillet 1962 règlementant l'entrée et le séjour des étrangers au Liban ainsi que leur sortie de ce pays* (Law of July 10, 1962, Regulating the Entry and Stay of Foreigners in Lebanon As Well as Their Departure from the Country).

[55] Human Rights Fist interview with Jordanian authorities, Amman, Jordan, April 19, 2010; Human Rights First interview with Lebanese authorities, Beirut, Lebanon, April 23, 2010.

[56] Egypt has made reservations to the following Articles Article 12 (personal status laws), Article 20 (rationing), Article 22 (1) (public education), Article 23 (public relief) and Article 24 (labor legislation and social security).

[57] Human Rights Fist interview with Jordanian authorities, Amman, Jordan, April 19th, 2010; Human Rights First interview with Lebanese authorities, Beirut, Lebanon, April 23, 2010.

[58] For example, see Egyptian Initiative for Personal Rights, *"Freedom of Belief and the Arrest of Shi'a Muslims in Egypt,"* April 2004, available at: http://eipr.org/en/report/2004/08/01/570, (accessed December 2, 2010)

[59] Mouna Abouissa, "Iraqi refugees in Egypt: living a nightmare," RT.com, February 6, 2009, available at: http://rt.com/Top_News/2009-02-06/iraqi_refugees_in_Egypt__living_a_nightmare.html, (accessed December 10, 2010).

[60] Human Rights First interview with Iraqi refugee in Amman, Jordan, April 17, 2010.

[61] Ibid.

[62] Human Rights First interview with Iraqi refugee in Amman, Jordan, April 21, 2010.

[63] Human Rights First interview with Iraqi refugee in Cairo, Egypt May 24, 2010.

[64] Human Rights First interview with legal aid organization, Jordan, April 18, 2010.

[65] In Jordan, for example, UNHCR has identified additional families in need of cash assistance however resources available do not allow an increase in the number of beneficiaries, see U.N.OCHA, "Regional Response Plan for Iraqi Refugees, 2010 Mid-Year Review" available at http://ochaonline.un.org/humanitarianappeal/webpage.asp?Page=1887, (accessed December 2, 2010), p. 38.

[66] Nicholas Seeley, " The Politics of Aid to Displaced Iraqis in Jordan," Middle East Report, vol. 256, (Fall 2010), pp. 37-42.

[67] Human Rights First interview with St. Andrews Resettlement Legal Aid Project, Cairo, Egypt, March 31, 2010.; Human Rights First interview with AMERA Egypt, Cairo, Egypt, July 11, 2010.

[68] Human Rights First interview with St. Andrews Resettlement Legal Aid Project, Cairo, Egypt, March 31, 2010.

[69] Human Rights First interview with UNHCR staff, Amman, Jordan, April 15, 2010. See also: AFP, "U.N. suspends medical aid to Iraqi families in Jordan," July 21, 2009, available at: http://www.google.com/hostednews/afp/article/ALeqM5g1glKjexzYOwwwnJ-qq5W27yONeA (accessed December 10, 2010) and U.N.OCHA, " Regional Response Plan," p. 1.

[70] UNOCHA, " Regional Response Plan Mid-Year review," p. 1.

[71] UNHCR Lebanon, "Monthly Detention Report," October 2010, on file with Human Rights First.

[72] Ibid.

[73] Ibid.

[74] Human Rights First email correspondence with UNHCR Damascus, Syria, August 23, 2010; Human Rights First email correspondence with UNHCR Damascus, Syria, December 9, 2010.

[75] Human Rights First interview with UNHCR staff, Amman, Jordan, April 15, 2010.

[76] Human Rights First interview with Iraqi refugee, Amman, Jordan April 17 2010.

[77] Human Rights First interview with Iraqi refugee, Amman, Jordan April 17 2010.

[78] Human Rights First interview with Center for Victims of Torture, Amman, Jordan, April 18, 2010.

[79] For example, see Human Rights Watch, They Want Us Exterminated: Murder, Torture, Sexual Orientation and Gender in Iraq, (New York: Human Rights Watch: August 2009), available at http://www.hrw.org/node/85050, (accessed December 10, 2010), pp. 53-57.

[80] UNOCHA, " Regional Response Plan," p. 1.

[81] The UNHCR's criteria for determining resettlement eligibility are contained in Chapter 4 of its Resettlement Handbook. In addition, a March 2007 UNHCR document which sets forth UNHCR's resettlement policy for Iraqi refugees from central and southern Iraq outlines 11 profiles of Iraqi refugees who will be prioritized for resettlement submissions. Though many of these criteria are the same as those found in the UNHCR Resettlement Handbook, additional criteria included are specific to Iraqi refugees, for example, Iraqis who fled as a result of their association in Iraq with the Multi National Forces. The policy paper is available at: http://www.unhcr.org/45f80f9d2.pdf, (accessed December 2, 2010).

[82] USRAP, "Information Sheet, Refugee Resettlement in the United States" available at http://www.jordan.iom.int/Doc/Attachment%202010-06%20Final%20USRAP%20information%20sheet%20April%2030%20(2).pdf, (accessed December 10, 2010).

[83] UNHCR, "U.N. chief announces 100,000 landmark in resettlement of Iraqi refugees," June 18, 2010, available at: http://www.unhcr.org/4c1b17b56.html (accessed July 22, 2010).

[84] As of the end of July 2010, the U.S. had resettled 49,306 Iraqi refugees, see figures from WRAPS available at http://www.wrapsnet.org/Reports/AdmissionsArrivals/tabid/211/language/en-US/Default.aspx, (accessed December 13, 2010)

[85] From fiscal year 2007 to November of fiscal year 2011, the U.S. has admitted 55,278 Iraqi refugees—see http://www.wrapsnet.org/Reports/AdmissionsArrivals/tabid/211/language/en-US/Default.aspx, (accessed December 10, 2010).

[86] UNHCR, "U.N. chief announces 100,000 landmark in resettlement of Iraqi refugees," June 18, 2010, available at: http://www.unhcr.org/4c1b17b56.html, (accessed December 10, 2010).

[87] Ibid.

[88] See endnote 6.

[89] Civil society meeting with National Security Council on Iraqi refugees and IDPs, Washington, D.C., September 10, 2010; civil society meeting with Department of State officials on expedited resettlement, Washington, D.C., July 12, 2010.

[90] Eric P, Schwartz, Assistant Secretary, Bureau of Population, Refugees and Migration. "Remarks Before the Commission on Security and Cooperation in Europe," Washington D.C., July 22, 2010, available at http://www.state.gov/g/prm/rls/rmks/2010/145455.htm, (accessed December 13, 2010).

[91] The names of all Iraqis quoted in this report have been changed to protect their privacy and safety.

[92] Information provided by pro bono attorney working with U.S.-affiliated Iraqis to Human Rights First via email, November 2010.

[93] Spouses and unmarried children under age 21 may be included on the principal SIV application as derivative applicants. Ahmed aged out of eligibility to be included on his father's SIV application. See the State Department's FAQs at http://travel.state.gov/visa/immigrants/info/info_4172.html#3b, and Section 1244(b)(2)(A) of the National Defense Authorization Act for FY 2008 (Public Law 110-181).

[94] Information provided by *pro bono* attorney working with U.S.-affiliated Iraqis to Human Rights First via email, November 2010.

[95] Human Rights First interview with Iraqi refugee family, Amman, Jordan, April 17, 2010.

[96] For information on ongoing persecution experienced by religious minorities in Iraq, see Bureau of Democracy, Human Rights and Labor, Department of State, *International Religious Freedom Report, 2009* October 26, 2009, available at http://www.state.gov/g/drl/rls/irf/2009/127348.htm, accessed December 10, 2010). Also see endnote 7 above.

[97] While Human Rights First was interviewing IOM and the State Department's Refugee Coordinator in Amman, Jordan Human Rights First learned that certain families were asked to travel from Syria to Jordan if "there had been pressure for them to do so." Human Rights First was unable to obtain any further information about this issue during its interviews.

[98] Human Rights First interview with Iraqi refugee family, Amman, Jordan, April 17, 2010.

[99] Additional reasons for deferrals include the need to verify documents, clarify information with UNHCR or if relevant verify an applicant's relationship to a relative. See Appendix 1 for different versions of this letter.

[100] According to IOM Amman, in April 2010 there were 100 Iraqi cases deferred for nine months or more. Human Rights First interview with IOM Amman, Jordan, April 20, 2010.

[101] Human Rights First interview with Iraqi refugee family, Amman, Jordan, April 16, 2010.

[102] Human Rights First interview with UNHCR representative, Beirut, Lebanon, April 22, 2010.

[103] Human Rights First interview with Iraqi refugee family, Amman, Jordan, April 17 2010.

[104] Human Rights First interview with Iraqi refugee family, Amman, Jordan, April 17, 2010.

[105] Ibid.

[106] Ibid.

[107] Human Rights First interview with Iraqi refugee, New York, NY, May 19, 2010

[108] Ibid.

[109] Human Rights First interview with Iraqi refugee, New York, NY, June 9, 2010.

[110] Human Rights First interview with Iraqi refugee, New York, NY, May 24, 2010

[111] Human Rights First interview with UNHCR representatives, Washington D.C., June 10, 2010.

[112] Human Rights First interview with OPE representative, New York, NY, May 28, 2010.

[113] Human Rights First email correspondence with IOM representative, August 4, 2010.

[114] Department of Homeland Security, "Statement by Homeland Security Secretary Michael Chertoff on New Security Procedures for Processing Iraqi Refugees Seeking Resettlement in the United States," news release, May 29, 2007, available at http://www.dhs.gov/xnews/releases/pr_1180469448282.shtm, (accessed December 13, 2010).

[115] Criteria that determine which type of refugee requires an SAO remains classified. Stakeholders directly involved in resettlement processing informed Human Rights First that SAOs are required for all Iraqi male applicants age 14 to 66. Human Rights First was unable to confirm this information.

[116] Civil society meeting with National Security Council on Iraqi refugees and IDPs, Washington, D.C., September 10, 2010; civil society meeting with Department of State officials on expedited resettlement, Washington, D.C., July 12, 2010.

[117] On August 3, 2010 the Department of State informed Human Rights First via email that the average SAO processing time required for one individual Iraqi is 152 days. Yet one particular individual may require multiple SAOs conducted by different intelligence agencies. The Department also informed Human Rights First that it takes an average of only 38 days to process one individual SAO. As individuals require multiple SAOs, the longer processing time of 152 days required to complete an SAO for one individual is likely due to inadequate coordination and resources on the part of U.S. intelligence agencies.

[118] In his report, which was commissioned by the Department of State David Martin recommends that "the agencies involved need to assure continued full staffing of the SAO process so that all initial review will be completed within the stated time frames (currently forty-five days)." See David Martin, *The United States Refugee Admissions Program: Reforms for a New Era of Refugee Resettlement*, 2005, Migration Policy Institute, p. 90.

[119] David Martin, *The U.S. Refugee Admissions Program*, p. 72.

[120] U.S. Government Accountability Office, "Iraqi Refugee Assistance: Improvements Needed in Measuring Progress, Assessing Needs, Tracking Funds, and Developing an International Strategic Plan," April 2009, available at http://www.gao.gov/new.items/d09120.pdf (accessed December 13, 2010), p. 33.

[121] Ibid.

[122] USCIS Ombudsman, "Recommendation Regarding ...Refugee Status," p. 5. .

[123] Human Rights First, *Promises to the Persecuted, p. 15.*

[124] The List Project to Resettle Iraqi Allies *Tragedy on the Horizon: A History of Just and Unjust Withdrawal*, May 2010, available at http://thelistproject.org/Withdrawal.pdf (accessed November, 2, 2010), p. 29.

[125] Ibid.

[126] Human Rights First meeting with Department of State representative, Washington, D.C., July 20, 2010.

[127] Press release, "Levin Applauds Inclusion of Iraqi Refugee Legislation in Defense Bill Conference Report," December 7, 2007, available at http://levin.senate.gov/newsroom/release.cfm?id=288555 (accessed December 14, 2010).

[128] Includes translators who worked for the U.S. government or military, staff hired to work on USAID and other State Department contracts, staff hired to work on Department of Defense reconstruction efforts, Iraqis working on USAID-sponsored programs, and others. Congressional Budget Office, "Contractors' Support of U.S. Operations in Iraq," August 2008, available at http://www.cbo.gov/ftpdocs/96xx/doc9688/08-12-IraqContractors.pdf (accessed December 13, 2010), table 1, p. 9.

[129] Human Rights First, *Promises to the Persecuted*," p. 19.

[130] George Packer, "Betrayed," *The New Yorker*, March 2007, and Spencer Hsu, "Envoy Urges Visas for Iraqis Aiding the U.S.," *Washington Post*, July 22, 2007.

[131] In August 2010, Kirk Johnson, whose organization, The List Project to Resettle Iraqi Allies, has directly assisted hundreds of U.S.-affiliated Iraqis since 2007, told Human Rights First: "Despite the fluctuations in daily violence, there has been little to no decline in the lethal stigma and hazards presented by working alongside the U.S. military or government and its contractors. As bases are shuttered, thousands of these Iraqis are now being 'cut loose,' without any protection, at a time of increasing violence and targeted assassinations by terrorist groups such as the Islamic State of Iraq, which has expressly stated its intent to target U.S.-affiliated Iraqis in the wake of America's withdrawal."

[132] Tim Arango, "Iraq's Conflict, Reflected in a Family Tragedy," *New York Times*, July 19, 2010, available at http://www.nytimes.com/2010/07/20/world/middleeast/20samarra.html?hp, (accessed December 13, 2010).

[133] Case example provided by a *pro bono* attorney who works with U.S.-affiliated Iraqis, November 2010.

[134] Human Rights First telephone interview with former Ambassador Ryan Crocker, November 30, 2010.

[135] Human Rights First, *Promises to the Persecuted*, p. 11.

[136] Press statement, Senator Edward Kennedy (D-MA), "Provisions provide refugee status for Iraqis associated with the United States who are under threat of persecution," December 7, 2007, available at http://www.allamericanpatriots.com/48738702_kennedy-smith-levin-brownback-iraqi-refugee-provisions-defense-authorization-conference-rep (accessed December 14, 2010).

[137] See remarks by Senator Gordon Smith (R-OR) before the U.S. Commission on International Religious Freedom hearing entitled "Sectarian Violence in Iraq and the Refugee Crisis," September 19, 2007, available at http://www.uscirf.gov/component/content/article/160-iraq-press-releases/2158-hearing-on-sectarian-violence-in-iraq-and-the-refugee-crisis-remarks-by-senator-gordon-smith-r-or.html (accessed December 14, 2010).

[138] Press release, "Levin Applauds Inclusion of Iraqi Refugee Legislation in Defense Bill Conference Report," December 7, 2007, available at http://levin.senate.gov/newsroom/release.cfm?id=288555 (accessed December 14, 2010).

[139] President Obama, "Responsibly Ending the War in Iraq."

[140] P2 eligibility is detailed in Section 1243(a) of the National Defense Authorization Act for FY 2008 (Public Law 110-181).

[141] The refugee definition in U.S. law includes individuals in their home country when designated by the President (INA 101(a)(42)(B)). In-country processing is rarely authorized for refugees, who by definition are individuals who have fled from their home country and sought refuge in another. In-country processing should never be treated as a substitute for providing asylum, or as a tool for urging refugees to return to a country where they would face persecution.

[142] The Department of State has not instituted P2 processing in Syria or Turkey as those countries will not permit the U.S. government to process refugees directly without the involvement of UNHCR.

[143] Human Rights First email correspondence with State Department official, September 8, 2010.

[144] Human Rights First, *Promises to the Persecuted*, p. 11.

[145] Human Rights First email correspondence with State Department official, September 10, 2010. On that date, there were 411 Iraqis in Egypt and 966 Iraqis in Jordan moving through the P2 process. In Iraq, the number was approximately 25,000.

[146] Human Rights First email correspondence with State Department official, July and August, 2010.

[147] Edward M. Kennedy (MA). *Congressional Record*, p. S15613 (December 14, 2007).

[148] The older 2006 SIV program remains operational, and provides 50 SIVs per year for Iraqi and Afghan interpreters and translators who worked for the U.S. government. It was mandated in Section 1059 of the National Defense Authorization Act for FY 2006 (Public Law 109-163).

[149] The 1244 SIV program was mandated in Section 1244 of the National Defense Authorization Act for FY 2008 (Public Law 110-181), part of a section known as the Refugee Crisis in Iraq Act. To be eligible for 1244 SIVs, Iraqis must have worked for the U.S. government, military, or contractors for at least a year since 2003—when the United States invaded Iraq.

[150] Eligibility requirements are described in Section 1244(b) of the National Defense Authorization Act for FY 2008 (Public Law 110-181). The applicant must also demonstrate faithful and valuable service to the U.S. government through a positive recommendation from his or her senior supervisor The earlier program—known as the Sec. 1059 program—has slightly different requirements; it is for translators only, there is no "ongoing serious threat" requirement as in the Sec. 1244 program, and applicants must present a letter of recommendation from a flag officer (a one-star to four-star general or admiral). The Sec. 1244 program is available to a broader range of U.S.-affiliated Iraqis and has additional evidentiary requirements.

[151] Section 1244(b)(2) of the National Defense Authorization Act for FY 2008 (Public Law 110-181). Children must be unmarried and under age 21.

[152] The 2006 program was mandated in Section 1059 of the National Defense Authorization Act for FY 2006 (Public Law 109-163).

[153] See State Department Fact Sheet data as of September 30, 2010 at http://www.travel.state.gov/pdf/SQNumbers0910.pdf (accessed December 14 2010).

[154] Human Rights First, *Promised to the Persecuted,* p. 11.

[155] Human Rights First email correspondence with State Department official, July and August, 2010.

[156] Human Rights First telephone interviews with *pro bono* attorneys, July 2010.

[157] Human Rights First, *Promises to the Persecuted*, p. 12.

[158] Human Rights First telephone interviews with *pro bono* attorneys July 2010; email correspondence with USCIS official, August 2010.

[159] Memo from *pro bono* attorneys and advocates with expertise relating to U.S.-affiliated Iraqis and NGO stakeholders, including Human Rights First, to Director for Human Rights, National Security Council, sent October 31, 2010.

[160] Human Rights First, *Promised to the Persecuted,* p. 12. For further discussion of COM approval delays, see Saurabh Sanghvi, "Abandoned in Baghdad," August 31, 2010, available at http://www.nytimes.com/2010/08/31/opinion/31sanghvi.html (accessed December 14, 2010).

[161] Partially in response to the recommendations memo (see endnote 159), a State Department official outlined several reforms to the process, some recently implemented, some planned for the future, in a meeting on November 30, 2010.

[162] As detailed in this section, this number includes 2,524 principal SIVs, 2,523 SIVs for spouses and children, and 7,649 Iraqi refugees resettled through the P2 process.

[163] Guy Goodwin Gil, The Refugee in International Law, Third Edition, (Oxford University Press, 2007), p. 499.

[164] UNHCR, "Information Note and Recommendations from UNHCR: Emergency Resettlement and the Use of Temporary Evacuation Transit Facilities," May 9, 2010, available at http://www.unhcr.org/refworld/docid/4bf3adfb2.html, (accessed December 2, 2010), p. 1.

[165] Currently, UNHCR conducts resettlement on three different priority levels: 1)*Emergency*, for cases where the immediacy of security and/or other acute life-threatening situation faced by the refugee in the country of asylum necessitates resettlement within a few days, if not hours; 2) *Urgent*, for refugees who have serious medical risks or other vulnerabilities requiring expedited resettlement within six weeks of submission; 3) *Normal*, for all cases where there are no immediate medical, social or security risks that would merit expedited processing. The majority of cases fall within the final category. UNHCR expects decisions and departure within 12 months of submission." See UNHCR, "Emergency Resettlement," p. 1.

[166] UNHCR "Emergency Resettlement," p. 1.

[167] In 2009, countries with emergency resettlement programs include: Brazil, Denmark, Finland, the Netherlands, Norway, New Zealand and Sweden. Other countries, including Australia and Canada, may consider on an exceptional basis and in certain circumstances emergency cases. Detailed discussion of U.S. policy and practice on emergency cases is included below.

[168] Human Rights First interview with Head, Resettlement Service, UNHCR Geneva, Switzerland, July 1, 2010.

[169] UNHCR further elaborates refugees in need of evacuation, see UNHCR, "Emergency Resettlement," p.2.

[170] Human Rights First interviews with UNHCR staff in Amman, Jordan on April 15 and April 21, 2010, and Beirut, Lebanon on April 22 and April 28, 2010.

[171] Human Rights First telephone interview with Canadian officials, Embassy of Canada, Damascus, Syria, April 18, 2010. This information was also confirmed with UNHCR Damascus via telephone interview on August 11, 2010.

[172] For additional information on Iraqi women in Jordan and Syria facing honor crimes and trafficking, see Sebastian Swett and Cameron Webster, "U.S. Dodges Obligation to Help Iraqi Women Trafficked into Sexual Slavery," *The Nation*, August 19, 2010, available at http://www.thenation.com/article/154080/us-dodges-obligation-help-iraqi-women-trafficked-sexual-slavery, (accessed November 30, 2010).

[173] Human Right First email correspondence with Geraldine Chatelard, December 8, 2010.

[174] See Human Rights Watch, *They Want Us Exterminated*, for further information.

[175] Human Rights first email correspondence with AMERA Egypt, June 2, 2010.

[176] For further information on the Egyptian authorities use of debauchery and homosexuals in Egypt, see Human Rights Watch, *In A Time of Torture: The Assault on Justice in Egypt's Crackdown on Homosexual Conduct*, (New York: Human Rights Watch: February 29, 2004), available at http://www.hrw.org/en/reports/2004/02/29/time-torture-0, (accessed December 2, 2010).

[177] Human Rights First email communication with refugee assistance organization, April 3, 2010

[178] As Hassan had a criminal record, he also experienced difficulty finding housing as landlords in Egypt regularly request to review criminal records before rental agreements are signed, Human Rights First email communication with refugee assistance organization April 3, 2010.

[179] Human Rights First email correspondence with Iraqi Refugee Assistance Program, November 4, 2010.

[180] Luckily for this refugee, a USCIS circuit ride was already planned to be in the country of first asylum and hence able to interview him relatively quickly following a resettlement referral from UNHCR.

[181] Human Rights First email correspondence with Iraqi Refugee Assistance Program, November 4, 2010.

[182] In 2007, it was envisaged by UNHCR that refugees at risk and in need of evacuation include: refugees at immediate risk of refoulement (based on a strict interpretation and verified by the Resettlement Service) or other acute, life-threatening situation, refugees kept in prolonged detention (although not for the commission of a crime/offence) who can only be released if resettled, sensitive / high profile refugees at risk (e.g. political and human rights activists, journalists and individuals of certain nationalities), refugees in need of resettlement for whom a resettlement country and/or UNHCR requires that their final destination for permanent resettlement not be disclosed to the country of first asylum and refugees who might be victims or witnesses of concern to the International Criminal Court or other international tribunal. See UNHCR, "Emergency Resettlement," pp. 2-3.

[183] Ibid. p 4.

[184] Ibid, p 5.

[185] Ibid. p 4.

[186] Ibid.

[187] Human Rights First email correspondence with UNHCR Geneva, Switzerland, August 3, 2010.

[188] UNHCR, "Emergency Resettlement," p. 7.

[189] Ibid.

[190] Ibid.

[191] Ibid.

[192] Human Rights First email correspondence with UNHCR Geneva, Switzerland, August 3, 2010.

[193] UNHCR, "Agreement between the Government of Romania, UNHCR and IOM, Regarding Temporary Evacuation to Romania of Persons in Urgent Need of International Protection and their Onward Resettlement," May 8, 2008, available at http://www.unhcr.org/refworld/type,MEMORANDA,,,4a7c221c2,0.html , (accessed December 13, 2010), article 2, paragraph 3.

[194] UNHCR, "Emergency Resettlement," p. 7.

[195] Ibid. See endnote 165 above for information on the difference between emergency and urgent resettlement.

[196] Ibid.

[197] Eric P. Schwartz, Assistant Secretary, Bureau of Population, Refugees, and Migration, Department of State, announced the formation of this group in remarks delivered at the Department of State's LGBT Pride Month Celebration, see "Protecting LGBT Asylum Seekers and Refugees," June 22, 2010, available at http://www.state.gov/g/prm/rls/rmks/2010/143751.htm, (accessed December 13, 2010).

[198] Proposed Refugee Admissions for Fiscal Year 2011, Report to the Congress.

[199] "Expediting Cases in the U.S. Refugee Admissions Program," distributed by Department of State representatives to civil society groups on July 12, 2010.

[200] Estimated Time Frames For Expedited Cases," distributed by Department of State representatives to civil society groups on July 12, 2010, on file with Human Rights First.

[201] "Expediting Cases in the U.S. Refugee Admissions Program."

[202] Ibid.

[203] Ibid.

[204] Human Rights First email correspondence with IOM Amman, Jordan, April 29, 2010.

[205] Ibid.

[206] See the U.S. Country Chapter in "UNHCR Resettlement Handbook," June 8, 2009, available at http://www.unhcr.org/pages/4a2ccba76.html , (accessed December 13, 2010).

[207] Ibid.

[208] In 2000, the U.S. introduced the "U.S. Protocol for Emergency Resettlement Cases referred by UNHCR" but according to the State Department this was superseded following governmental restructuring and other changes that took place in the following years, Human Rights First email correspondence with Department of State representative, March 8, 2010.

[209] USCIS Memorandum, "Response to Recommendation 44," p. 2

[210] USCIS Ombudsman, "Recommendation Regarding the Adjudication of Applications for Refugee Status," p. 1.

[211] USCIS Memorandum, "Response to Recommendation 44," p. 2.

[212] David Martin, The United States Refugee Admissions Program: Reforms for a New Era of Refugee Resettlement (Washington, D.C.: Migration Policy Institute, 2005), p.55.

[213] USCIS Ombudsman, "Recommendation Regarding the Adjudication of Applications for Refugee Status," p. 2.

[214] UNHCR, "Emergency Resettlement," p. 9.

[215] Civil society letter sent to Secretary Clinton on the urgent protection needs of LGBTI refugees, March 31, 2010, on file with Human Rights First.

[216] See above on page 38 where this is noted.

[217] "Expediting Cases in the U.S. Refugee Admissions Program."

[218] U.S. Department of State, Foreign Affairs Manual, Volume 9, Appendix 0/100, "Refugee Resettlement Policy," p. 2., available at http://www.state.gov/documents/organization/88040.pdf (accessed December 5, 2010).

[219] Human Rights First interview with Iraqi refugee in Amman, Jordan, April 20, 2010.

[220] Given the serious human rights violations and ongoing insecurity in Iraq, and most prominently in the five Central Governorates of Baghdad, Diyala, Kirkuk, Ninewa and Salah Al-Din, UNHCR continues to consider all Iraqi asylum seekers from these areas to be in need of international protection, and encourages a prima facie approach in those countries where the numbers of Iraqi asylum seekers is such that an individual determination is not feasible, see UNHCR, "Eligibility Guidelines for Assessing the International Protection Needs of Iraqi Asylum Seekers," April 2009, available at http://www.unhcr.org/refworld/docid/49f569cf2.html (accessed November 30, 2010). In July 2009, UNHCR affirmed the continued applicability of these guidelines, see UNHCR, "Note on the Continued Applicability of the April 2009 UNHCR Eligibility Guidelines for Assessing the International Protection Needs of Iraqi Asylum-Seekers," July 2010, available at http://www.unhcr.org/refworld/docid/49f569cf2.html, (accessed December 2, 2010)

221 UNHCR Press Release, "U.N. chief announces 100,000 landmark in resettlement of Iraqi refugees," June 18 2010, available at http://www.unhcr.org/4c1b17b56.html, (accessed December 13, 2010).

222 UNHCR's criteria for determining resettlement eligibility are contained in Chapter 4 of its Resettlement Handbook, available at http://www.unhcr.org/pages/4a2ccba76.html (accessed December 13, 2010). In addition, in March 2007 UNHCR outlined 11 profiles of Iraqi refugees who will be prioritized for resettlement submissions. All of these profiles are in line with and further contextualize UNHCR's global resettlement criteria found in its handbook, see UNHCR, "Resettlement of Iraqi Refugees," March 12, 2007, available at http://www.unhcr.org/45f80f9d2.pdf (accessed August 10, 2010).

223 For example, the U.S. requires that potential applicants meet the definition of a refugee found in the Immigration and Nationality Act, which closely follows the definition of the 1951 Convention, see U.S. Chapter of UNHCR's Resettlement Handbook. Other resettlement countries maintain similar requirements, available at http://www.unhcr.org/pages/4a2ccba76.html , (accessed December 13, 2010).

224 Human Rights First interviews with UNHCR staff in Cairo, Egypt, April 1, 2010, and Amman, Jordan, April 15 and April 21, 2010, and Beirut, Lebanon, April 22 and April 28, 2010.

225 Human Rights First interview with Iraqi refugee, Amman, Jordan, April 20, 2010.

226 Human Rights First interview with Iraqi refugee, Amman, Jordan, April 20, 2010.

227 Human Rights First interview with Iraqi refugee, Amman, Jordan, April 18, 2010.

228 UNHCR, "Convention and Protocol Relating to the Status of Refugees," Article 1F (a), (b), and (c).

229 UNHCR, "Surviving in the city: A review of UNHCR's operation for Iraqi refugees in urban areas of Jordan, Lebanon and Syria," July 2009, available at http://www.unhcr.org/4a69ad639.html , (accessed December 10, 2010) pp. 24-25.

230 Ibid.

231 Ibid.

232 UNHCR has developed exclusion criteria for Iraqi refugees yet this information remains confidential.

233 In two previous comprehensive studies, Human Rights First—then known as the Lawyers Committee for Human Rights—outlined what it means to conduct exclusion determinations in accordance with standards of procedural fairness, see, Lawyers Committee for Human Rights (now Human Rights First), *Refugees, Rebels and the Quest for Justice*," (New York: Lawyers Committee For Human Rights, 2002), chapter 5, part B, pp. 147-170.

234 UNHCR, "Surviving in the city," p. 24.

235 Human Rights First interview with UNHCR representatives, Washington, D.C. June 10, 2010 and Human Rights First interview with UNHCR representatives, Geneva, Switzerland, July 1, 2010.

236 Saltsman, Adam, *Facing an Uncertain Future: Improving CARE's capacity to provide displaced Iraqis in Jordan with information on resettlement and return,"* November 2009, pg 35.

237 Ibid.

238 USCIS Notice of Ineligibility, on file with HRF. Other reasons for denials based on credibility include "involvement in acts of persecution or your involvement in an entity known to commit acts of persecution," "status and/or resettlement in a third country," "admissibility to the United States" or "other."

239 USCIS Notice of Ineligibility, on file with HRF.

240 USCIS Ombudsman, "Recommendation Regarding the Adjudication of Applications for Refugee Status," p. 2.

241 Ibid, Pg 5.

242 Correspondence on file with Human Rights First.

243 In Fiscal Year 2009, 85.3 percent of the Iraqis who were interviewed were approved by the U.S., Human Rights First email correspondence with USCIS, August 13, 2010.

244 USCIS Notice of Ineligibility, on file with HRF.

245 USCIS, Factors to Keep in Mind When Evaluating Crediability, Lesson Plan, on file with Human Rights First.

246 In Fiscal Year 2009, USCIS informed HRF that 37.5% of Iraqi refugees denied resettlement were denied for reasons related to credibility, Human Rights First email correspondence with USCIS, August 13, 2010, on file.

247 Human Rights First interview with Iraqi refugee in Amman, Jordan, April 17, 2010.

248 See Immigration and Nationality Act (INA) § 208(b)(2)(i). The former version of the "Notice of Ineligibility" phrased this ground for denial in negative and in terms of legal burdens of proof, making it unintelligible to many native speakers of English who are not lawyers; the current version is clearer to an English reader but still provides no factual explanation.

249 Human Rights First interview with Iraqi refugee in Amman, Jordan, April 20, 2010.

250 Human Rights First interview with USCIS, Washington D.C., July 13, 2010.

251 Ibid.

252 Human Rights First email correspondence with USCIS, December 14, 2010.

253 USCIS Ombudsman, "Recommendation Regarding the Adjudication of Applications for Refugee Status," p. 3.

254 Ibid, p. 5.

255 USCIS Memorandum, "Response to Recommendation 44," p. 4.

256 Human Rights First interview with St. Andrews Resettlement Legal Aid Project, Cairo, Egypt, March 31, 2010. In addition, Human Rights First was informed that on multiple occasions legal representatives from the Iraqi Refugee Assistance Project requested to observe U.S. resettlement interviews and such requests were denied by officials from the Department of State.

257 Ibid.

258 USCIS Ombudsman, "Recommendation Regarding the Adjudication of Applications for Refugee Status," p. 2.

259 USCIS Memorandum, "Response to Recommendation 44," p. 5.

260 Ibid.

261 Refugee Council USA, "The U.S. Refugee Admissions and Resettlement Program at a Crossroads, Recommendations by Refugee Council USA."

262 President Obama noted this review as part of the proclamation he issued on World Refugee Day 2010 (June 18); a full text of this speech is available at http://www.whitehouse.gov/the-press-office/presidential-proclamation-world-refugee-day (accessed December 13, 2010) . This review is also cited in the Executive Summary of Columbia University's May 2010 report written at the request of the International Rescue Committee. See Columbia University School of International and Public Affairs, *Refugee Resettlement in the United States: An Examination of Challenges and Proposed Solutions* , (New York: Columbia University, May 2010) available at http://www.sipa.columbia.edu/academics/workshops/documents/IRCCapstoneworkshopSIPAcopy.pdf, p. iii, (accessed November 30, 2010).

263 Eric P, Schwartz, Assistant Secretary, Bureau of Population, Refugees and Migration. "Remarks Before the Commission on Security and Cooperation in Europe," Washington D.C., July 22, 2010, available at http://www.state.gov/g/prm/rls/rmks/2010/145455.htm, (accessed December 13, 2010).

264 *Ibid.*

265 Human Rights First interviews with Iraqi refugees, New York, New York, May 14–June 28, 2010. During these interviews, Human Rights First met with two Iraqis processed in Cairo, Egypt who received no CO prior to departure. Another Iraqi interviewed for this report noted that his CO in Damascus, Syria was taught by someone who had never been to the U.S. and that the cost-of-living in the U.S. was never addressed.

266 RCUSA, along with all the voluntary agencies who are recipients of this grant, have applauded the increase in funds for the Reception & Placement program.

267 Bureau of Population, Refugees and Migration, U.S. Department of State, "Doing Right by Newly Arrived Refugees," *news release,* January 22, 2010, available at http://www.state.gov/g/prm/rls/news/136429.htm (accessed December 5, 2010).

268 Proposed Refugee Admissions for Fiscal Year 2011, Report to the Congress.

269 Georgetown University Law Center, *Refugee Crisis in America: Iraqis and their Resettlement Experience (Washington D.C.: Georgetown University Law Center, October 2009),* available at http://www.law.georgetown.edu/news/releases/documents/RefugeeCrisisinAmerica_000.pdf, (accessed December 13, 2010), p. 21.

270 Human Rights First interview with resettled Iraqi refugee, New York, New York, June 25, 2010.

271 The 2010 Refugee Protection Act, legislation introduced by Senator Patrick Leahy (D-VT) on March 15, 2010, would require the Secretary of State to adjust the reception and placement grant each year for inflation and cost of living increase, see *Leahy Introduces Landmark Refugee Protection Act,* March 2010, available at http://leahy.senate.gov/press/press_releases/release/?id=ea7b1d65-e893-4998-b121-65ab874eaf8b (accessed November 15, 2010).

[272] Achieving Self-sufficiency: Refugee Assistance and Employment, Refugee Council USA Policy Paper, on file with Human Rights First.

[273] Ibid.

[274] Georgetown University Law Center, *Refugee Crisis in America, p. 39.*

[275] Columbia University, *Refugee Resettlement in the United States,* p. 15. This reports notes that "money allocated to volags by the federal government to cover the initial resettlement period does not follow the refugee upon secondary migration."

[276] This recommendation is echoed in the International Rescue Committee's June 2009 report. See International Rescue Committee, *Iraqi Refugees in the United States: In Dire Straits*, (New York: International Rescue Committee, June 2009), available at http://www.theirc.org/sites/default/files/resource-file/irc_report_iraqcommission.pdf (accessed December 13, 2010), p. 10. The report emphasizes that "the 'one size fits all' approach of insisting on early employment is not necessarily the best policy for many refugees, the resettlement program, or American society [...] many Iraqi refugees arrive with high levels of educational and professional experience. To make best use of the talents and skills they possess, funds need to be spent on recertification programs to ensure that refugees can enter the workforce as professionals. This is in the best interest of both there refugees and the communities that welcome them."

[277] U.S. Department of Health and Human Services, *Office of Refugee Resettlement,* "Matching Grant," available at http://www.acf.hhs.gov/programs/orr/programs/match_grant_prg.htm (accessed December 13, 2010).

[278] Upwardly Global (see website at http://www.upwardlyglobal.org/) is located in San Francisco, New York City and Chicago. RefugeeWorks (see website at http://www.refugeeworks.org/) is located in Baltimore. Both organizations work with refugees and asylees at no cost to assist in professional recertification.

[279] *International Organization for Migration,* "Refugee Travel Loans," available at http://www.iom.int/jahia/Jahia/activities/pid/1392, (accessed December 13, 2010).

[280] The recommendation to temporarily suspend refugee travel loans was also proposed in IRC's *Dire Straits* report. IRC further recommends that "suspension of the practice of reporting to credit bureaus delinquencies in the repayment of refugee travel loans. Negative reports may further compromise the ability of refugees to obtain jobs," p. 13.

www.ingramcontent.com/pod-product-compliance
Lightning Source LLC
Chambersburg PA
CBHW051421200326
41520CB00023B/7319